D1246126

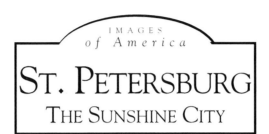

IMAGES
of America

ST. PETERSBURG
THE SUNSHINE CITY

The Sunshine City
by CLARK DeBALL

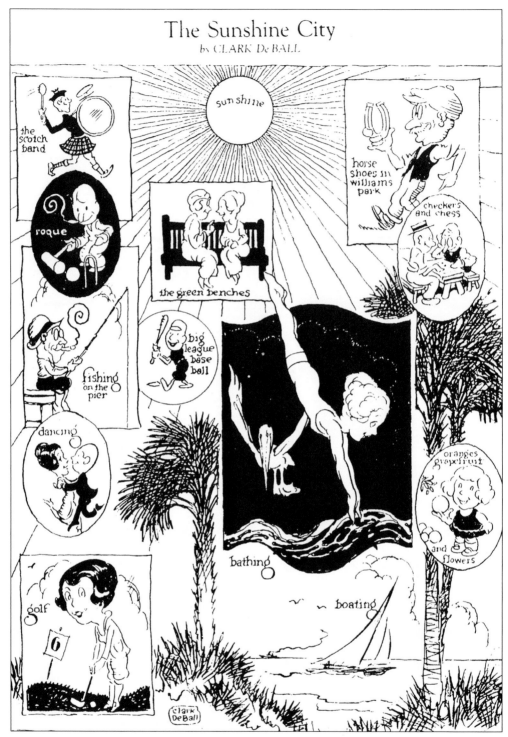

Everything under the sun . . . that is what St. Petersburg, Florida promised tourists during the boom era. Perpetual sunshine was the major draw but an abundance of activities and attractions made St. Petersburg the place to be.

IMAGES
of America

ST. PETERSBURG
THE SUNSHINE CITY

R. Wayne Ayers

ARCADIA
PUBLISHING

Published by Arcadia Publishing
Charleston SC , Chicago IL, Portsmouth NH, San Francisco CA

Printed in the United States of America

Library of Congress Catalog Card Number: 2001087614

For all general information contact Arcadia Publishing at:
Telephone 843-853-2070
Fax 843-853-0044
E-Mail sales@arcadiapublishing.com
For customer service and orders:
Toll-Free 1-888-313-2665

Visit us on the Internet at www.arcadiapublishing.com

DEDICATION

To my wife, Nancy, whose creative spark and tireless toil have made this book a reality.

CONTENTS

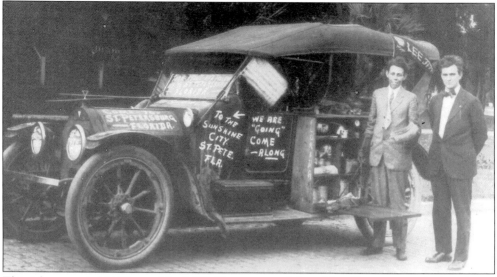

This jalopy carried "Alligator Man" Bill Carpenter and friend Joe Honey on a whirlwind tour of the country in 1916, during which Carpenter wrestled his alligator "Trouble" and touted St. Petersburg to potential tourists. Carpenter, a flamboyant promoter, owned the Royal Palm Theater and an adjacent gift shop where he shipped baby alligators and performed tricks with Trouble.

ACKNOWLEDGMENTS

The author wishes to express his appreciation for the generous support given by the Pinellas County Historical Society and the St. Petersburg Historical Society, especially to the following:

Ken Ford, museum director, Heritage Village–Pinellas County Historical Museum; and Don Ivey, curator of collections

Holly McConnell, curator of education, St. Petersburg Museum of History; and Ann Wikoff, archivist

The author consulted a number of sources in writing the captions for this book. He found the following books to be especially helpful and recommends them to anyone wanting an in-depth look at area history:

Arsenault, Raymond. *St. Petersburg and the Florida Dream, 1888–1950.* Gainesville, FL: University Press of Florida, 1996.
Baker, Rick. *Mangroves to Major League.* St. Petersburg, FL: Southern Heritage Press, 2000.
Grismer, Karl H. *The Story of St. Petersburg.* St. Petersburg, FL: P.K. Smith & Company, 1948.
Hurley, Frank T. Jr. *Surf, Sand, & Post Card Sunsets.* Printed by Precision Litho Service, Inc., 1989.
Marth, Del R. and Martha J. *St. Petersburg: Once upon a Time.* Branford, FL: Suwannee River Press, 1996.

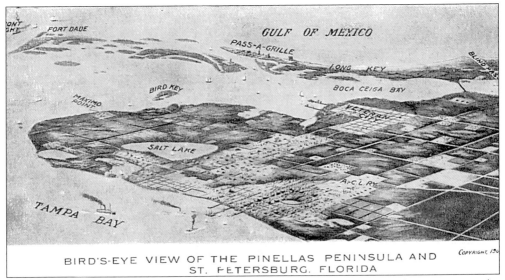

BIRD'S-EYE VIEW OF THE PINELLAS PENINSULA AND ST. PETERSBURG, FLORIDA

This early relief map shows the area as it appeared in 1909. The primary development was in the St. Petersburg area, spreading inward from Tampa Bay.

INTRODUCTION

Boom era promoter Lew B. Brown developed "The Sunshine City" theme to showcase St. Petersburg's prime attraction—year-round balmy sunshine. To back his claim, Brown, also editor of the *Evening Independent*, offered free newspapers any day the sun didn't shine. He paid off less than five times a year during the paper's 57-year run.

The Sunshine City slogan took off, and the tourists came. They came, by rail, steam, or auto, and found a land of tropical splendor waiting for them . . . with wonders to behold and deals too good to pass up.

Lavish hotels and country clubs rose up to court the well-to-do, with guesthouses and tourist courts ready for the less affluent. Shuffleboard, roque, golf, chess, dog racing, and nightclubbing filled days and nights with exercise and excitement; parks and gardens were places to stroll and behold; the famous green benches provided relaxation and neighborliness; and water, water everywhere beckoned bathers and sun worshippers. Real estate salesmen, in their trademark knickers, were ready to offer the deal of a lifetime to anyone wanting a share of paradise.

St. Petersburg, The Sunshine City, was a city built on tourism and that legacy remains today, in the beautiful bayfront, meticulously restored hotels, Mediterranean Revival architecture, lovingly cared for parks and gardens, and the graceful ambiance of the city. Hospitality and friendliness are still the order of the day, though the green benches were removed in the 1950s in an effort to cast the city in a more youthful light. The sun still shines nearly every day even though the newspaper that guaranteed it is gone. The swells of visitors return every year to seek the sun . . . and many remain, giving area real estate a continuing boost.

With its radiant tropical beauty, blue skies, and sunny laid-back disposition, St. Petersburg was, and remains, The Sunshine City.

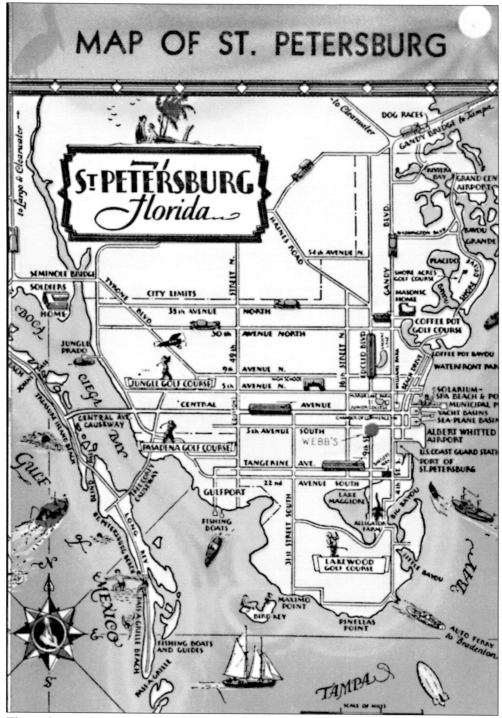

MAP OF ST. PETERSBURG

St.PETERSBURG *florida*

This early map shows many of the sights and attractions that brought tourists to St. Petersburg.

One

PROMOTING THE SUNSHINE CITY

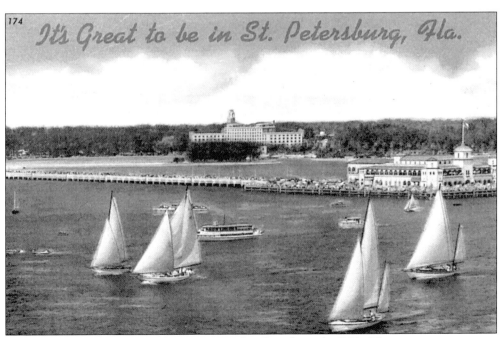

This card says it was "Great to be in St. Petersburg" in the early 1900s. The scene captures some of the major attractions St. Petersburg held for the tourists: sailing, boating, fishing, a Million-Dollar Pier, lavish hotels, and a magnificent climate allowing year-round enjoyment of it all.

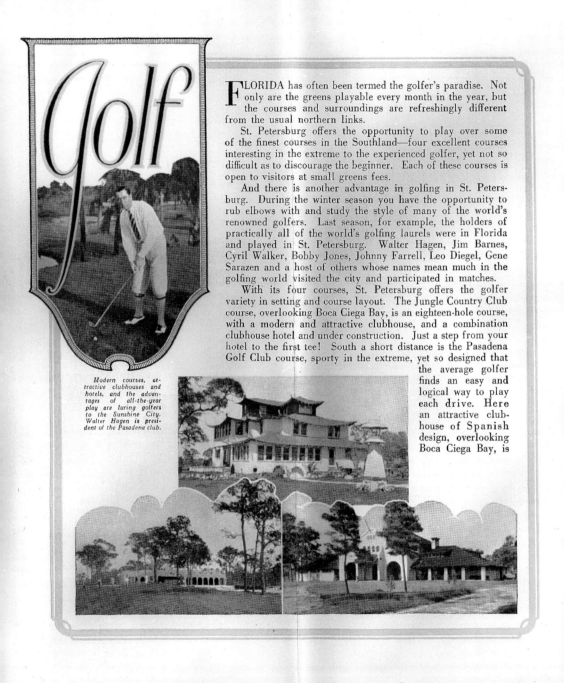

Golf

FLORIDA has often been termed the golfer's paradise. Not only are the greens playable every month in the year, but the courses and surroundings are refreshingly different from the usual northern links.

St. Petersburg offers the opportunity to play over some of the finest courses in the Southland—four excellent courses interesting in the extreme to the experienced golfer, yet not so difficult as to discourage the beginner. Each of these courses is open to visitors at small greens fees.

And there is another advantage in golfing in St. Petersburg. During the winter season you have the opportunity to rub elbows with and study the style of many of the world's renowned golfers. Last season, for example, the holders of practically all of the world's golfing laurels were in Florida and played in St. Petersburg. Walter Hagen, Jim Barnes, Cyril Walker, Bobby Jones, Johnny Farrell, Leo Diegel, Gene Sarazen and a host of others whose names mean much in the golfing world visited the city and participated in matches.

With its four courses, St. Petersburg offers the golfer variety in setting and course layout. The Jungle Country Club course, overlooking Boca Ciega Bay, is an eighteen-hole course, with a modern and attractive clubhouse, and a combination clubhouse hotel and under construction. Just a step from your hotel to the first tee! South a short distance is the Pasadena Golf Club course, sporty in the extreme, yet so designed that the average golfer finds an easy and logical way to play each drive. Here an attractive clubhouse of Spanish design, overlooking Boca Ciega Bay, is

Modern courses, attractive clubhouses and hotels, and the advantages of all-the-year play are luring golfers to the Sunshine City. Walter Hagen is president of the Pasadena club.

St. Petersburg was aptly termed a "Golfer's Paradise," offering the ideal climate for year-round play. This 1924 promotional brochure boasts "courses and surroundings that are refreshingly under construction, and a new hotel adjacent to the course will be open during the 1925-26 season.

Still farther south but within the city, is the Lakewood course, laid out in the form of a huge butterfly, and here play may be watched at every hole from motor cars, winding boulevards lining the greens and fairways. The first unit of a large clubhouse has been completed.

Along the northern shore section of Tampa Bay is the Coffee Pot course, with both an eighteen and a nine-hole course and an attractive clubhouse. This course has been improved from time to time and it is now one of the most popular of the city's links.

The greens on all four courses are grass greens, and the fairways are long stretches of greensward, with a sprinkling of water hazards and sand traps and rough to make each course distinctive and interesting.

Within one hour's motoring distance of St. Petersburg are more than a half dozen other attractive courses where play may be arranged. But no golfer need seek greater variety or more sporty chances—or better "everyday" golf —than may be enjoyed on the four courses within the city limits of the Sunshine City.

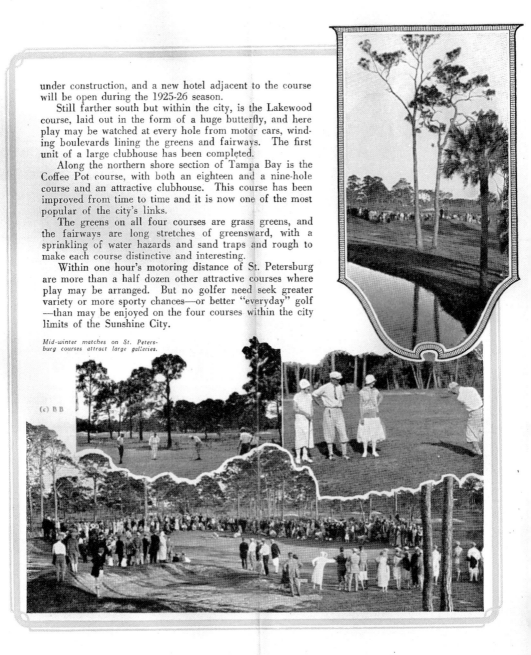

Mid-winter matches on St. Petersburg courses attract large galleries.

(c) B B

different from northern links." Many of the golf "greats" of the day—Walter Hagen, Gene Sarasen, and Bobby Jones—regularly played St. Petersburg courses.

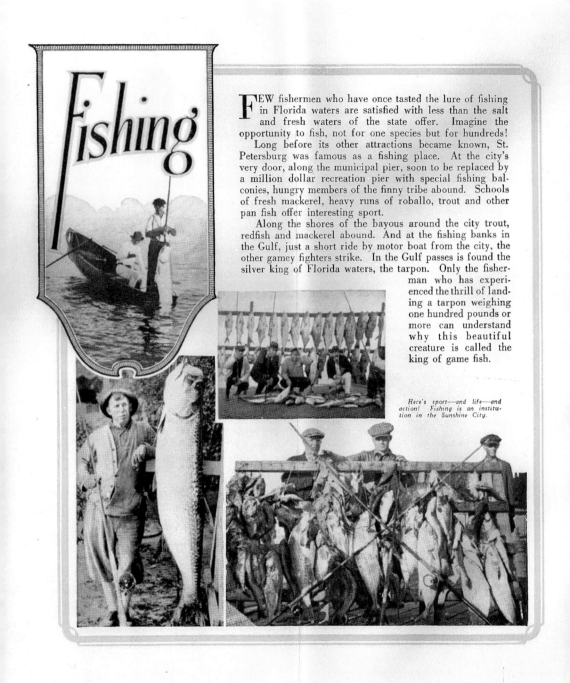

Fishing

FEW fishermen who have once tasted the lure of fishing in Florida waters are satisfied with less than the salt and fresh waters of the state offer. Imagine the opportunity to fish, not for one species but for hundreds!

Long before its other attractions became known, St. Petersburg was famous as a fishing place. At the city's very door, along the municipal pier, soon to be replaced by a million dollar recreation pier with special fishing balconies, hungry members of the finny tribe abound. Schools of fresh mackerel, heavy runs of roballo, trout and other pan fish offer interesting sport.

Along the shores of the bayous around the city trout, redfish and mackerel abound. And at the fishing banks in the Gulf, just a short ride by motor boat from the city, the other gamey fighters strike. In the Gulf passes is found the silver king of Florida waters, the tarpon. Only the fisherman who has experienced the thrill of landing a tarpon weighing one hundred pounds or more can understand why this beautiful creature is called the king of game fish.

Here's sport—and life—and action! Fishing is an institution in the Sunshine City.

Attracted by the multitudes of fish in the area, Spaniards established "fishing ranchos" along the Pinellas Coast long before the white settlers arrived. In fact, Pinellas Point was shown as Fisherman's Point on early maps. Fishing provided a good livelihood to Spanish fishermen who carried on a lucrative business with the fish markets in Cuba.

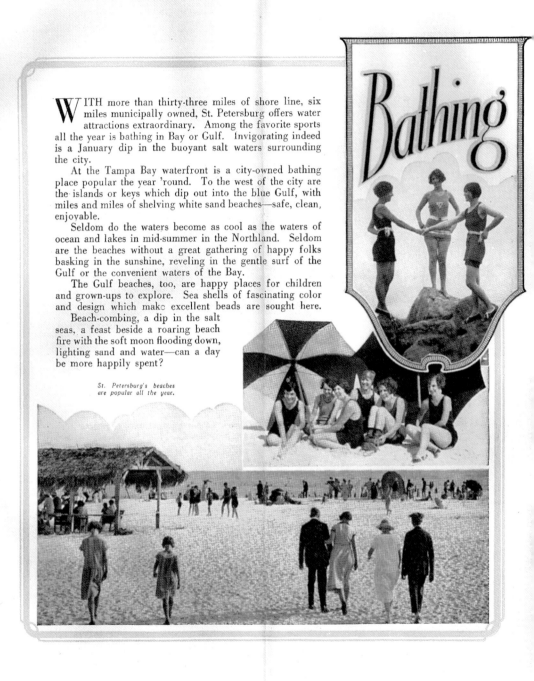

W ITH more than thirty-three miles of shore line, six miles municipally owned, St. Petersburg offers water attractions extraordinary. Among the favorite sports all the year is bathing in Bay or Gulf. Invigorating indeed is a January dip in the buoyant salt waters surrounding the city.

At the Tampa Bay waterfront is a city-owned bathing place popular the year 'round. To the west of the city are the islands or keys which dip out into the blue Gulf, with miles and miles of shelving white sand beaches—safe, clean, enjoyable.

Seldom do the waters become as cool as the waters of ocean and lakes in mid-summer in the Northland. Seldom are the beaches without a great gathering of happy folks basking in the sunshine, reveling in the gentle surf of the Gulf or the convenient waters of the Bay.

The Gulf beaches, too, are happy places for children and grown-ups to explore. Sea shells of fascinating color and design which make excellent beads are sought here.

Beach-combing, a dip in the salt seas, a feast beside a roaring beach fire with the soft moon flooding down, lighting sand and water—can a day be more happily spent?

St. Petersburg's beaches are popular all the year.

Sun bathing was a prime attraction in the Sunshine City. The warm, hospitable climate was especially appealing to Northerners during the frozen winter months, and St. Petersburg could offer "more than thirty-three miles of shoreline" featuring "water attractions extraordinaire."

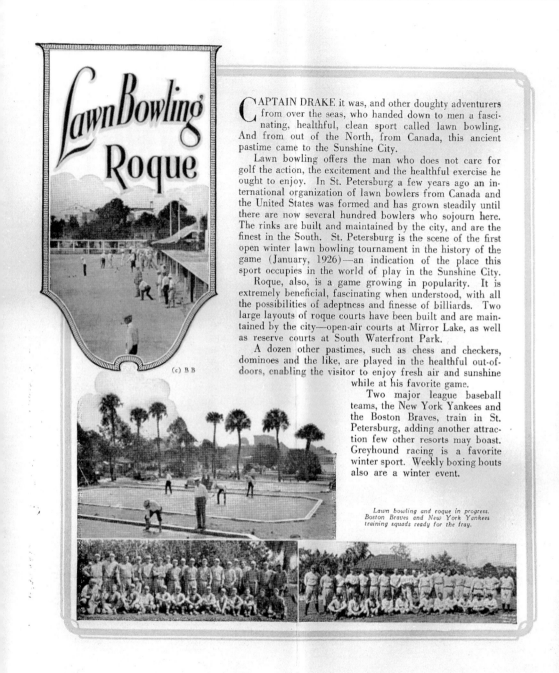

Lawn Bowling Roque

(c) B B

CAPTAIN DRAKE it was, and other doughty adventurers from over the seas, who handed down to men a fascinating, healthful, clean sport called lawn bowling. And from out of the North, from Canada, this ancient pastime came to the Sunshine City.

Lawn bowling offers the man who does not care for golf the action, the excitement and the healthful exercise he ought to enjoy. In St. Petersburg a few years ago an international organization of lawn bowlers from Canada and the United States was formed and has grown steadily until there are now several hundred bowlers who sojourn here. The rinks are built and maintained by the city, and are the finest in the South. St. Petersburg is the scene of the first open winter lawn bowling tournament in the history of the game (January, 1926)—an indication of the place this sport occupies in the world of play in the Sunshine City.

Roque, also, is a game growing in popularity. It is extremely beneficial, fascinating when understood, with all the possibilities of adeptness and finesse of billiards. Two large layouts of roque courts have been built and are maintained by the city—open-air courts at Mirror Lake, as well as reserve courts at South Waterfront Park.

A dozen other pastimes, such as chess and checkers, dominoes and the like, are played in the healthful out-of-doors, enabling the visitor to enjoy fresh air and sunshine while at his favorite game.

Two major league baseball teams, the New York Yankees and the Boston Braves, train in St. Petersburg, adding another attraction few other resorts may boast. Greyhound racing is a favorite winter sport. Weekly boxing bouts also are a winter event.

Lawn bowling and roque in progress. Boston Braves and New York Yankees training squads ready for the fray.

Lawn bowling and roque were sedate, sophisticated sports that appealed to the more mature tourists who came to St. Petersburg for the winter. St. Petersburg was host to the nation's first lawn bowling tournament, held in January 1926. Roque, similar to croquet, was actually invented in St. Petersburg.

MORE than seven hundred members have been enrolled in the St. Petersburg Shuffleboard Club in less than a year. Perhaps nothing else could attest the popularity of this sport so well as the mere quotation of these figures. Men and women, boys and girls, enjoy the game immensely. Almost everybody is familiar with shuffleboard and how it enlivens the monotony of life aboard ocean liners. Here it is one more event in a round of pleasures.

There is another sport which has long been a favorite in the Sunshine City during the winter months, especially among visitors from the Middle West, where it is regarded in high favor. Men and women play it. Boys are adept at it. The game is horseshoe pitching.

Perhaps it strikes you as a homely sort of game. Yet it is as scientific as any other sport. Here you may become acquainted with its niceties, enjoy the fruits of healthful exercise, and perhaps become a dyed-in-the-wool horseshoe pitcher! Incidentally, the national horseshoe tournament for 1926 is a mid-winter Sunshine City event.

Tennis? Yes, the city has municipally owned tennis courts for the tennis player. Nearby there's a playground being built especially for growing boys and girls, too. These playgrounds, as well as the school playgrounds, are under the supervision of the city recreation board.

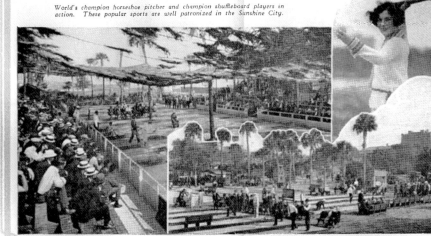

World's champion horseshoe pitcher and champion shuffleboard players in action. These popular sports are well patronized in the Sunshine City.

Shuffleboard was immensely popular, both as a spectator and participant sport, among early tourists. The St. Petersburg Shuffleboard Club enrolled more than 700 members in less than a year when it was founded in the mid-1920s and soon became the largest club in the world. Horseshoe pitching, too, was an inclusive sport of the era, being a favorite of men, women, and boys.

Parks

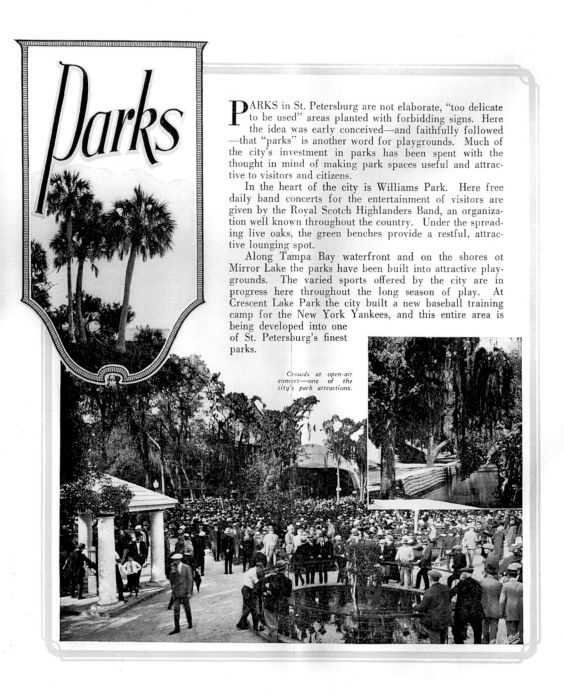

PARKS in St. Petersburg are not elaborate, "too delicate to be used" areas planted with forbidding signs. Here the idea was early conceived—and faithfully followed—that "parks" is another word for playgrounds. Much of the city's investment in parks has been spent with the thought in mind of making park spaces useful and attractive to visitors and citizens.

In the heart of the city is Williams Park. Here free daily band concerts for the entertainment of visitors are given by the Royal Scotch Highlanders Band, an organization well known throughout the country. Under the spreading live oaks, the green benches provide a restful, attractive lounging spot.

Along Tampa Bay waterfront and on the shores of Mirror Lake the parks have been built into attractive playgrounds. The varied sports offered by the city are in progress here throughout the long season of play. At Crescent Lake Park the city built a new baseball training camp for the New York Yankees, and this entire area is being developed into one of St. Petersburg's finest parks.

Crowds at open-air concert—one of the city's park attractions.

St. Petersburg took full advantage of its tropical climate and waterfront setting to develop a number of attractive parks and green areas, which gave the city its lush, tranquil atmosphere.

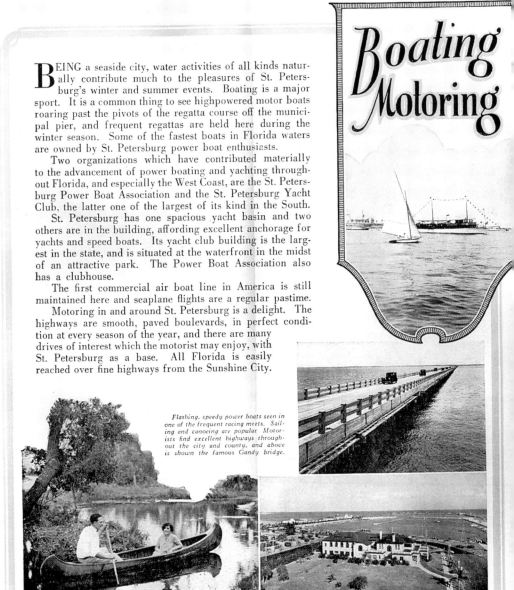

Boating
Motoring

BEING a seaside city, water activities of all kinds naturally contribute much to the pleasures of St. Petersburg's winter and summer events. Boating is a major sport. It is a common thing to see highpowered motor boats roaring past the pivots of the regatta course off the municipal pier, and frequent regattas are held here during the winter season. Some of the fastest boats in Florida waters are owned by St. Petersburg power boat enthusiasts.

Two organizations which have contributed materially to the advancement of power boating and yachting throughout Florida, and especially the West Coast, are the St. Petersburg Power Boat Association and the St. Petersburg Yacht Club, the latter one of the largest of its kind in the South.

St. Petersburg has one spacious yacht basin and two others are in the building, affording excellent anchorage for yachts and speed boats. Its yacht club building is the largest in the state, and is situated at the waterfront in the midst of an attractive park. The Power Boat Association also has a clubhouse.

The first commercial air boat line in America is still maintained here and seaplane flights are a regular pastime.

Motoring in and around St. Petersburg is a delight. The highways are smooth, paved boulevards, in perfect condition at every season of the year, and there are many drives of interest which the motorist may enjoy, with St. Petersburg as a base. All Florida is easily reached over fine highways from the Sunshine City.

Flashing, speedy power boats seen in one of the frequent racing meets. Sailing and canoeing are popular. Motorists find excellent highways throughout the city and county, and above is shown the famous Gandy bridge.

The automobile was coming of age during the boom era of the 1920s, while boats of all types were becoming faster and sleeker, making boating and motoring major recreational sports of the day. Challenging roads and sometimes-treacherous sea passages, plus the joy of racing, helped make both activities true "sport" during the early tourist days.

Hotels and Apartments

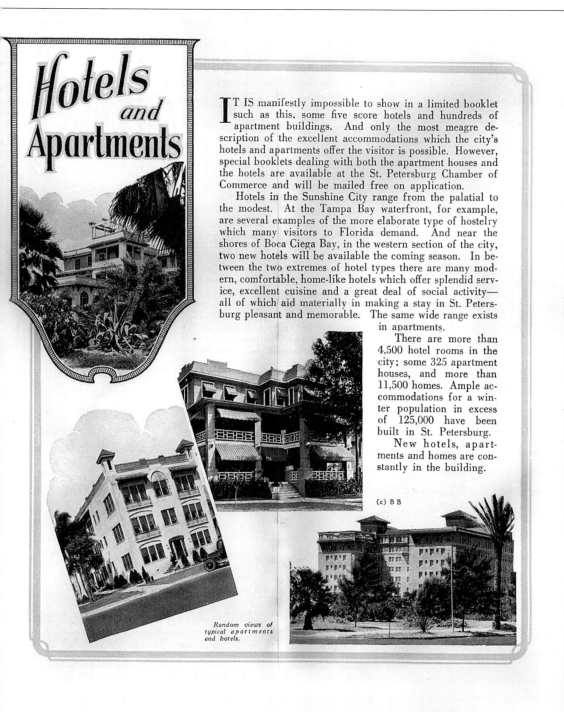

IT IS manifestly impossible to show in a limited booklet such as this, some five score hotels and hundreds of apartment buildings. And only the most meagre description of the excellent accommodations which the city's hotels and apartments offer the visitor is possible. However, special booklets dealing with both the apartment houses and the hotels are available at the St. Petersburg Chamber of Commerce and will be mailed free on application.

Hotels in the Sunshine City range from the palatial to the modest. At the Tampa Bay waterfront, for example, are several examples of the more elaborate type of hostelry which many visitors to Florida demand. And near the shores of Boca Ciega Bay, in the western section of the city, two new hotels will be available the coming season. In between the two extremes of hotel types there are many modern, comfortable, home-like hotels which offer splendid service, excellent cuisine and a great deal of social activity—all of which aid materially in making a stay in St. Petersburg pleasant and memorable. The same wide range exists in apartments.

There are more than 4,500 hotel rooms in the city; some 325 apartment houses, and more than 11,500 homes. Ample accommodations for a winter population in excess of 125,000 have been built in St. Petersburg.

New hotels, apartments and homes are constantly in the building.

(c) B B

Random views of typical apartments and hotels.

Developers rushed in to accommodate the tourist hordes by erecting a number of large, fashionable hotels and scores of smaller tourist courts and apartment houses. During one three-year span, ten major hotels were built. By the mid-1920s, St. Petersburg had over 5,000 hotel rooms.

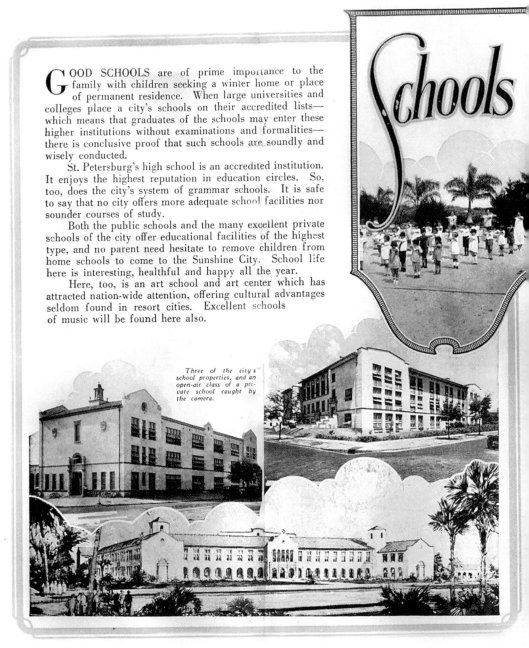

Schools

GOOD SCHOOLS are of prime importance to the family with children seeking a winter home or place of permanent residence. When large universities and colleges place a city's schools on their accredited lists—which means that graduates of the schools may enter these higher institutions without examinations and formalities—there is conclusive proof that such schools are soundly and wisely conducted.

St. Petersburg's high school is an accredited institution. It enjoys the highest reputation in education circles. So, too, does the city's system of grammar schools. It is safe to say that no city offers more adequate school facilities nor sounder courses of study.

Both the public schools and the many excellent private schools of the city offer educational facilities of the highest type, and no parent need hesitate to remove children from home schools to come to the Sunshine City. School life here is interesting, healthful and happy all the year.

Here, too, is an art school and art center which has attracted nation-wide attention, offering cultural advantages seldom found in resort cities. Excellent schools of music will be found here also.

Three of the city's school properties, and an open-air class of a private school caught by the camera.

The influx of new residents brought a demand for quality educational facilities. St. Petersburg responded by developing an excellent system of secondary schools, institutions of higher learning, and top-grade facilities offering education in specialties such as art and music.

Homes

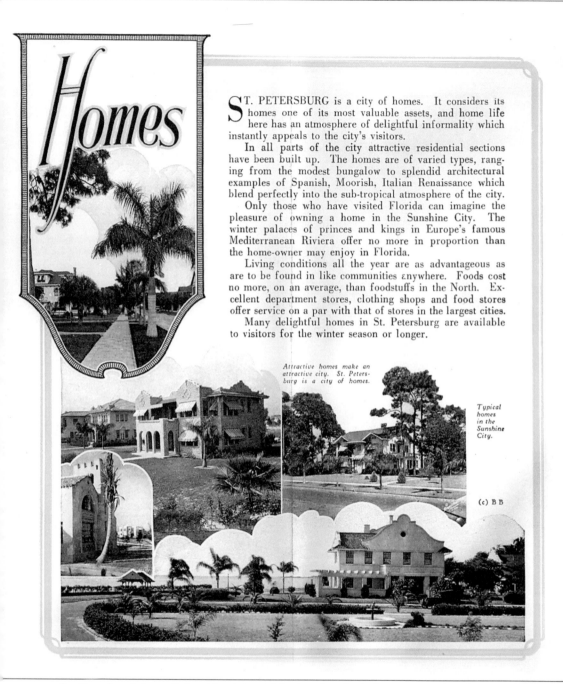

ST. PETERSBURG is a city of homes. It considers its homes one of its most valuable assets, and home life here has an atmosphere of delightful informality which instantly appeals to the city's visitors.

In all parts of the city attractive residential sections have been built up. The homes are of varied types, ranging from the modest bungalow to splendid architectural examples of Spanish, Moorish, Italian Renaissance which blend perfectly into the sub-tropical atmosphere of the city.

Only those who have visited Florida can imagine the pleasure of owning a home in the Sunshine City. The winter palaces of princes and kings in Europe's famous Mediterranean Riviera offer no more in proportion than the home-owner may enjoy in Florida.

Living conditions all the year are as advantageous as are to be found in like communities anywhere. Foods cost no more, on an average, than foodstuffs in the North. Excellent department stores, clothing shops and food stores offer service on a par with that of stores in the largest cities.

Many delightful homes in St. Petersburg are available to visitors for the winter season or longer.

Attractive homes make an attractive city. St. Petersburg is a city of homes.

Typical homes in the Sunshine City.

(c) B B

St. Petersburg's beautiful residential neighborhoods, which feature varied architectural styles complementing the area's lush landscaping, remain a vital part of the city's attractiveness. During the boom period, developers created entire neighborhoods from reclaimed swampland, building impressive homes in Spanish, Moorish, Italian Renaissance, and other styles that blended with the tropical surroundings. Many are still standing today in beautifully restored neighborhoods surrounding downtown.

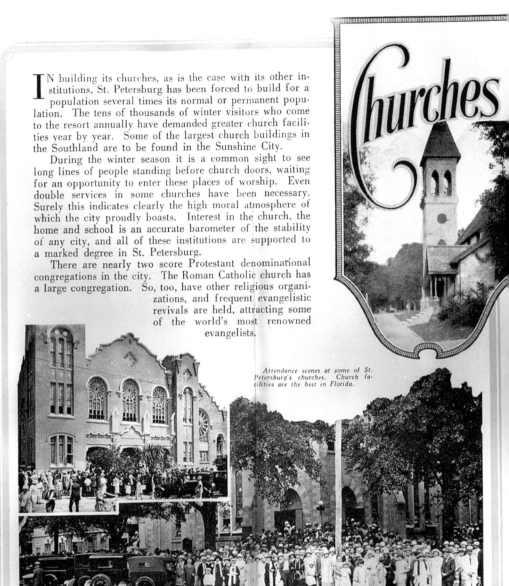

IN building its churches, as is the case with its other institutions, St. Petersburg has been forced to build for a population several times its normal or permanent population. The tens of thousands of winter visitors who come to the resort annually have demanded greater church facilities year by year. Some of the largest church buildings in the Southland are to be found in the Sunshine City.

During the winter season it is a common sight to see long lines of people standing before church doors, waiting for an opportunity to enter these places of worship. Even double services in some churches have been necessary. Surely this indicates clearly the high moral atmosphere of which the city proudly boasts. Interest in the church, the home and school is an accurate barometer of the stability of any city, and all of these institutions are supported to a marked degree in St. Petersburg.

There are nearly two score Protestant denominational congregations in the city. The Roman Catholic church has a large congregation. So, too, have other religious organizations, and frequent evangelistic revivals are held, attracting some of the world's most renowned evangelists.

Attendance scenes at some of St. Petersburg's churches. Church facilities are the best in Florida.

Karl Grismer, in his book *The Story of St. Petersburg*, describes the city as a "good town, whose winter visitors never cared for night life, carousing, or gambling. They were temperate, home-loving people who went to church regularly back North and intended to do the same while in St. Petersburg." As a result some of the largest churches in the South were built in St. Petersburg, and during the tourist season, long lines of people could be seen waiting for the church doors to open.

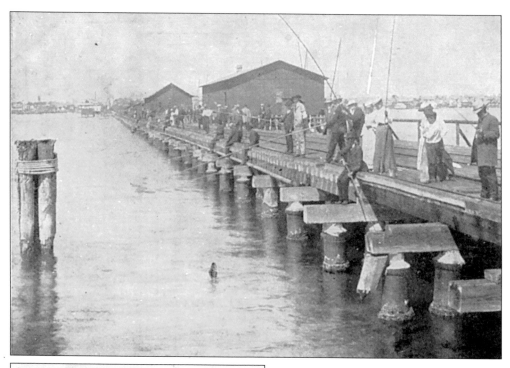

This ad card (both front and back are shown) from the early 1900s describes St. Petersburg as "The Tourist's Paradise . . . The Homeseeker's Refuge . . . The Land of Now and the Country of Splendid Realities."

Two

DOWNTOWN

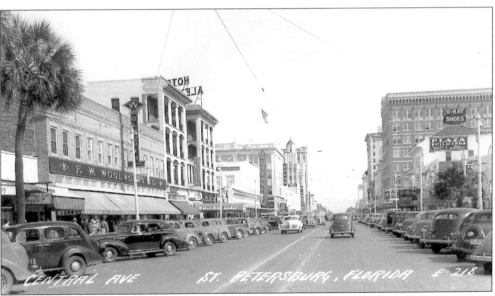

Many landmarks can be viewed in this 1930s look down bustling Central Avenue, including the Plaza Theater, Snell Arcade (the Rutland Building), Woolworth's, McCrory's, Kress, the Hotel Alexander, and the Pheil Building.

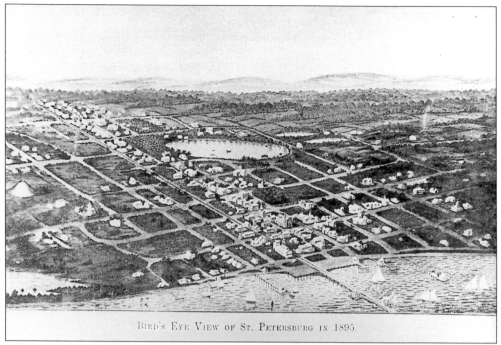

BIRD'S EYE VIEW OF ST. PETERSBURG IN 1895.

In this 1895 rendering, St. Petersburg is beginning to show its initial growth after the coming of Peter Demens's Orange Belt Railway in 1888. The town was named after Demens's native city in Russia. He drew straws with city founder John C. Williams for naming honors. Note Mirror Lake in the foreground.

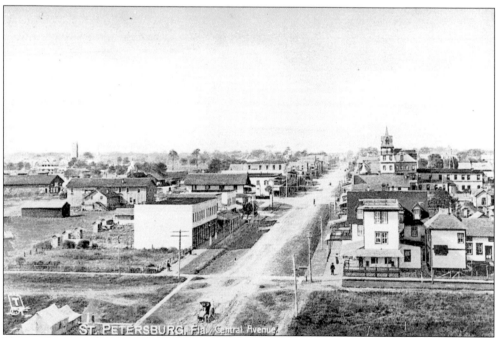

ST. PETERSBURG, Fla., Central Avenue.

This early print shows Central Avenue from Beach Drive in 1912. The rutted, sandy streets made travel difficult for both carriages and pedestrians.

24

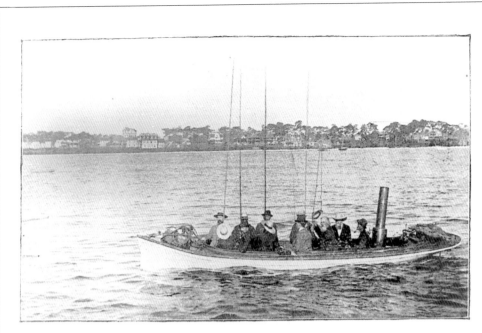

ST. PETERSBURG FROM THE HARBOR.

A boating party cruises St. Petersburg's Harbor in a crude steamboat.

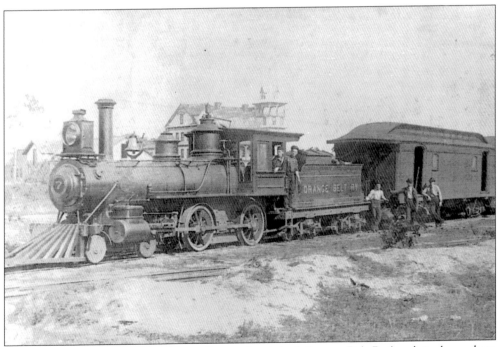

The *Shoo-Fly Special*, a train of Peter Demens's original Orange Belt Railroad, is shown here c. 1890 with the Detroit Hotel visible in the background.

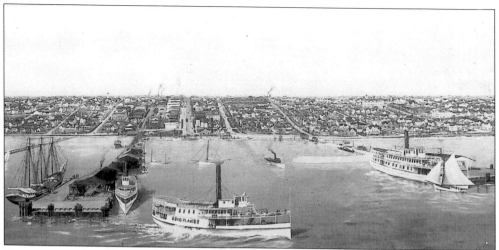

Tourists arrived at St. Petersburg by steamboat before the railroads opened the city up to the boom era. This scene from a 1907 painting by William Straub shows the steamer *H.B. Plant* in the foreground and the *Favorite* at dock on the right.

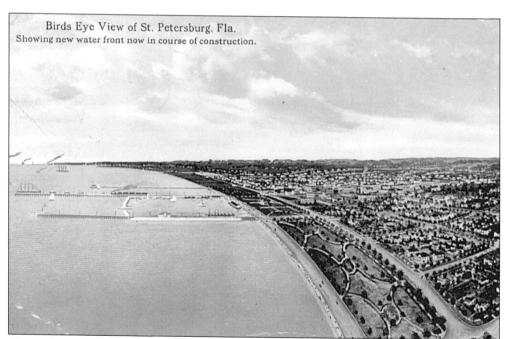

Birds Eye View of St. Petersburg, Fla.
Showing new water front now in course of construction.

This early rendering of the waterfront shows the railroad pier, boat traffic, and parkland along the shore.

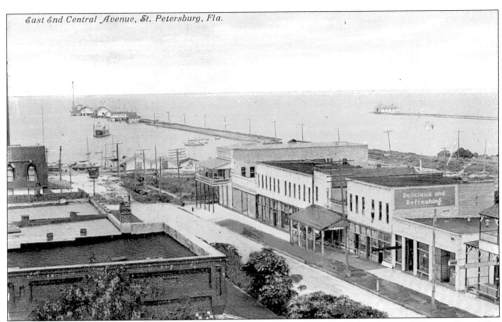

This scene from the mid-1910s shows the end of Central Avenue at the shore of Tampa Bay. The Municipal Pier, constructed in 1913, appears in the center.

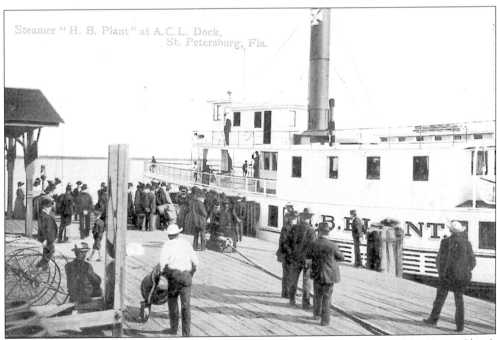

Steamer "H. B. Plant" at A.C.L. Dock, St. Petersburg, Fla.

The steamer *H.B. Plant* is busy loading passengers at the ACL Dock, owned by Henry Plant's Atlantic Coast Line Railroad. Rail lines were laid into the dock to facilitate connections between rail and steam lines.

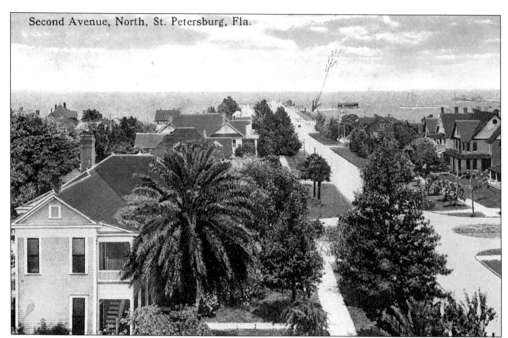

Second Avenue, North, St. Petersburg, Fla.

A bird's-eye view, looking toward the waterfront down Second Avenue North, shows that much of downtown in the 1920s had a residential character. The arrow points to the "2,800 ft. Pier where we landed." The writer adds, "The city is full of beautiful trees like these which adds much to the appearance of the streets. Most of the streets are laid out like this."

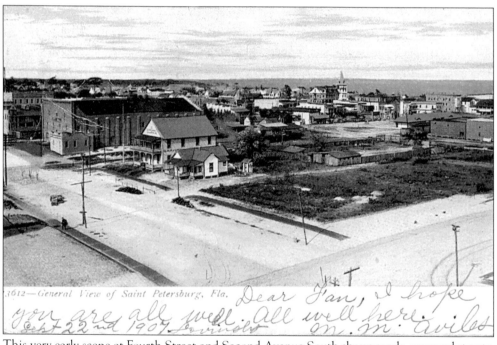

3612—General View of Saint Petersburg, Fla.

This very early scene at Fourth Street and Second Avenue South shows sandy, unpaved streets and much vacant land waiting to be developed. The city hall is the large brick building on the left; the two-story building with verandas is the Grand Army of the Republic (GAR) Hall.

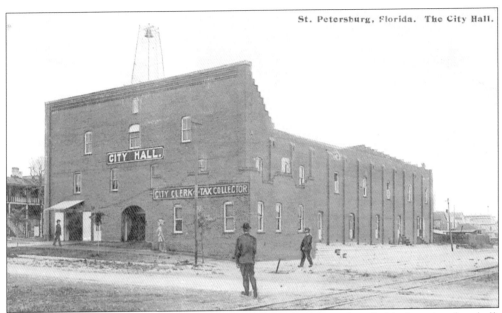

This view of city hall shows the tower atop the building that held the city fire bell. In 1906, St. Petersburg City Hall was moved from a shed to this massive structure, which was originally built as a manual training school annex by city benefactor E.H. Tomlinson.

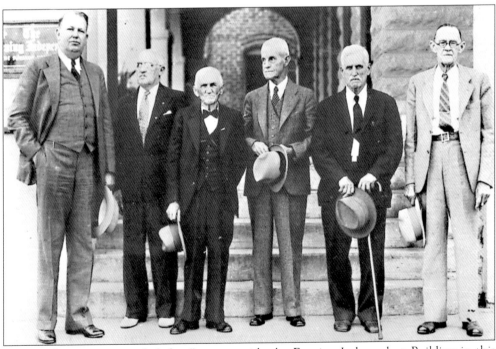

St. Petersburg "movers and shakers" pose outside the Evening Independent Building in this 1912 photograph. They are, from left to right, Dixie Hollins (first school superintendent), an unidentified man, A.F. Bartlett (pioneer booster), C.W. Weicking (first clerk of courts in Pinellas County), Jefferson T. Lowe (county commissioner), and T.J. Northrup (pioneer merchant, mayor of Clearwater, and the county's first tax assessor).

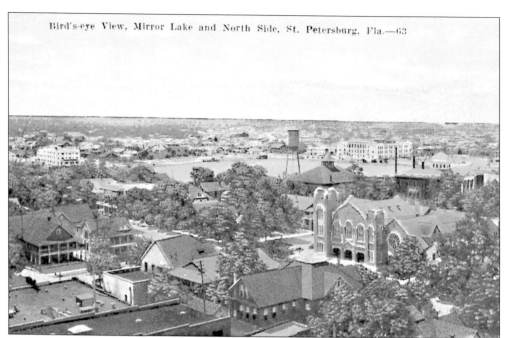

This view shows the development around Mirror Lake on the north side. The First Avenue Methodist Episcopal Church can be seen in the foreground at right. In 1923, the Suwannee Hotel was built across the street beside the church (see page 64).

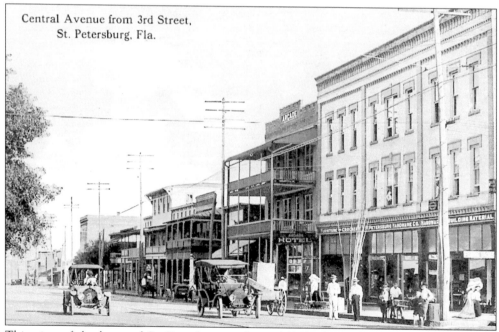

Central Avenue from 3rd Street, St. Petersburg, Fla.

This view of the heart of St. Petersburg in the mid-1910s shows the Arcade Hotel and the St. Petersburg Hardware Company. Note the wide verandas on nearly all buildings.

30

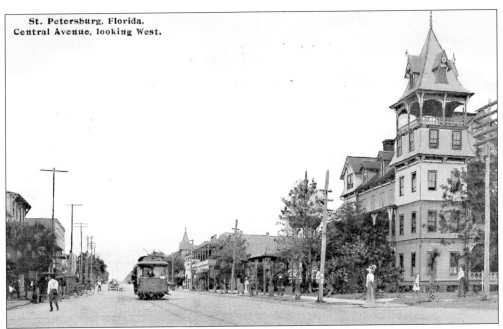

St. Petersburg, Florida.
Central Avenue, looking West.

This 1910 scene looking west down Central Avenue pictures three early means of transportation—buggies to the left, a vintage motorcar, and a streetcar. The massive structure on the corner is the Detroit Hotel.

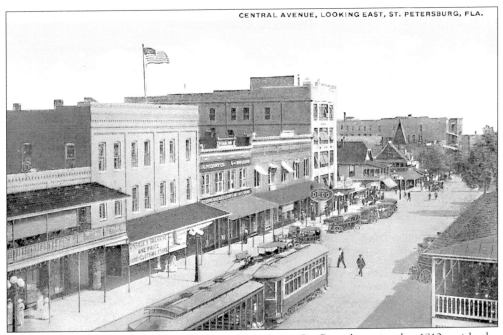

CENTRAL AVENUE, LOOKING EAST, ST. PETERSBURG, FLA.

This view down Central Avenue features downtown St. Petersburg in the 1910s with the remodeled "towerless" Detroit Hotel in the distance. Note the small T.G. McCrory's store with "nothing over 10 cents."

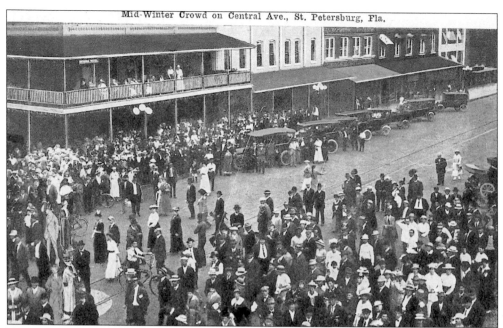

Mid-Winter Crowd on Central Ave., St. Petersburg, Fla.

Tourists jam Central Avenue downtown during the height of the winter season. The wide verandas of the Ansonia Hotel on the corner provided a shady spot for sitting and people watching.

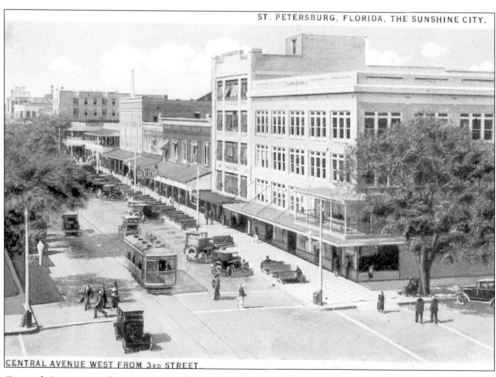

Central Avenue in the 1910s reveals awnings on every building and rows of sparsely populated green benches, which were to become a symbol of St. Petersburg hospitality (see next chapter).

The Home *of* Cheerful Service

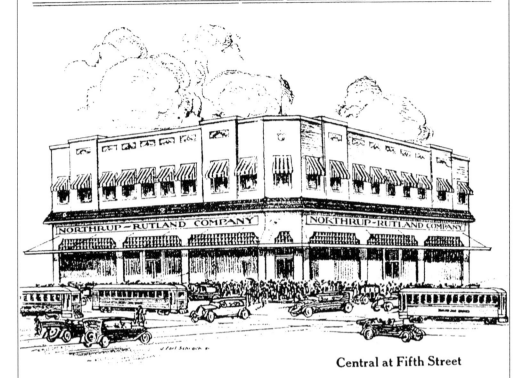

Central at Fifth Street

¶ If there is a virtue in the world of business that always helps, it is cheerful service. Willingly and cheerfully doing a thing doubles the worth of the deed. Cheerfulness promotes prosperity, creates harmony and increases efficiency.

¶ This air of cheerful service permeates throughout the Northrup-Rutland establishment. It is radiated by 75 cheerful sales experts, most of whom have been with the company since its opening.

¶ This alone should warrant your visiting this department store not to mention the quality of their goods, completeness of their stock, and the exceptional values they offer.

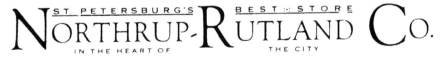

Rutland's Department Store, at Fifth and Central, touted itself as "St. Petersburg's Best Store."

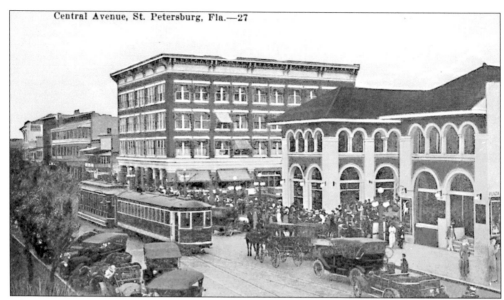

The La Plaza Theater, on the right, became the center of St. Petersburg culture after its opening in 1913. Built by George S. Gandy of Gandy Bridge fame and boasting the largest stage south of Atlanta, the structure hosted vaudeville acts, opera, and later, first-run movies. The building on the far left with the veranda was the Hotel Poinsettia, one of the boom-era hotels that catered to the well-to-do. Note the jammed streets.

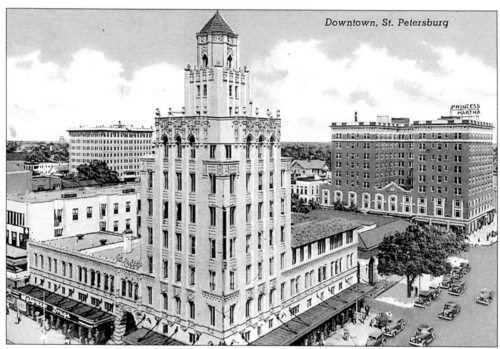

The Snell Arcade, later the Rutland Building, was the pride of developer Perry Snell and was described as the most beautiful building in downtown St. Petersburg. The design, by architects Richard Kiehnel and M. Leo Elliott of Miami, featured European statuary and mosaics. The building today remains a proud anchor of Fourth and Central, the heart of downtown.

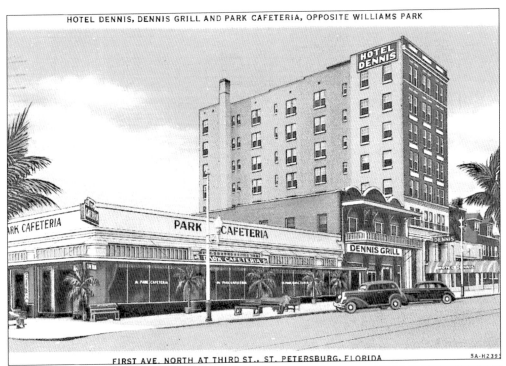

FIRST AVE. NORTH AT THIRD ST., ST. PETERSBURG, FLORIDA

5A-H239

Eateries were common downtown in early St. Petersburg. Pictured in these 1930s cards are the Park Cafeteria (especially popular during the money-scarce Depression years) and Hotel Dennis Grill, which served a more affluent clientele.

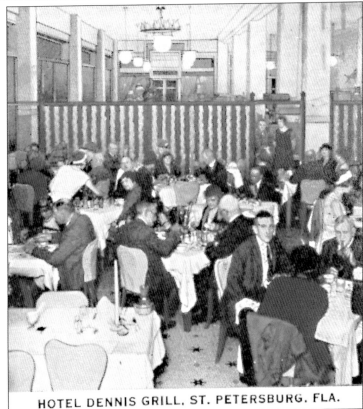

HOTEL DENNIS GRILL, ST. PETERSBURG, FLA.

35

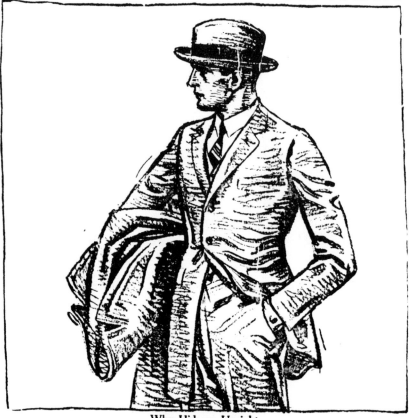
For fashionable dress, shoppers could choose Shepard & Co., featuring specially designed suits for the "erect man."

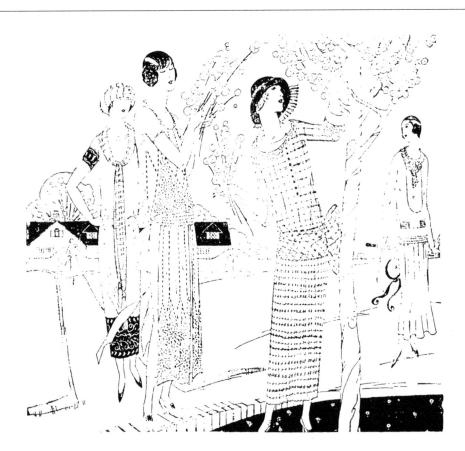

STYLE - VALUE - SERVICE

A trio of significant words-- the definite features of Mitchell success

E. L. Mitchell & Co.

"Correct Apparel For Women"

Ground Floor First National Bank Building

472-474-476 Central Avenue   St. Petersburg, Florida

Women could select the latest styles from E.L. Mitchell & Co., down the block from Shepard's, which touted "correct apparel for women."

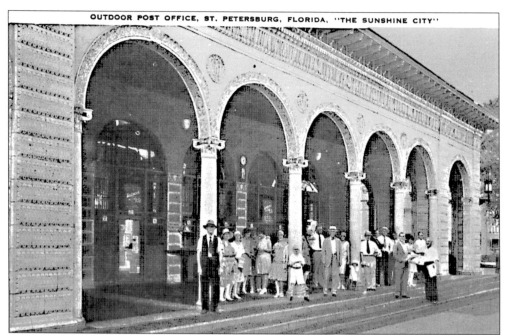

The Sunshine City erected the nation's only open-air post office, described as "sheltered only by a roof," in 1907. It was replaced in 1917 by this beautiful structure at First Avenue North and Fourth Street. Judging by the crowd waiting here, the open-air post office was a big success!

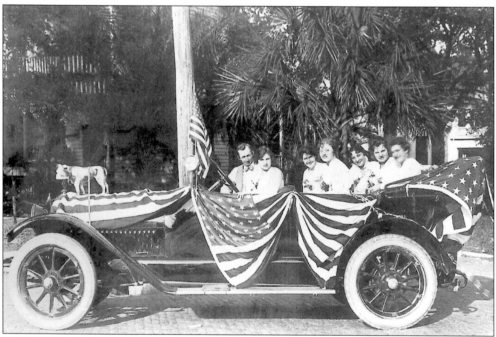

This flag-bedecked convertible with bulldog "hood ornament" was ready to lead the Festival of States Parade. The driver is Arthur L. Johnson, one of the founders of the festival and a prominent downtown businessman. The event has been an institution in St. Petersburg since 1917 and continues today.

38

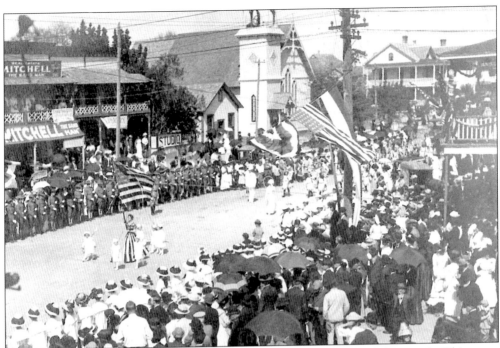

Predecessor to the Festival of States was the annual Washington's Birthday parade. This scene of the parade route down Central Avenue includes Mitchell's Corner, at Fourth and Central, where Noel Mitchell placed the original "green benches—then painted orange—to attract patrons to his real estate offices.

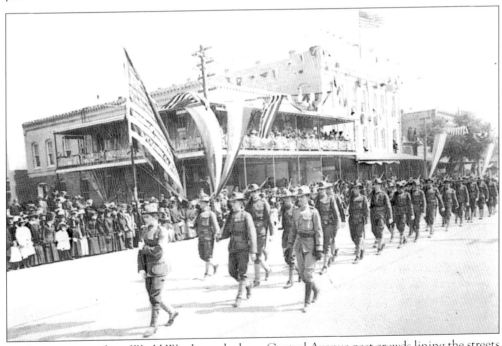

Soldiers returning from World War I parade down Central Avenue past crowds lining the streets and the veranda of the Ansonia Hotel.

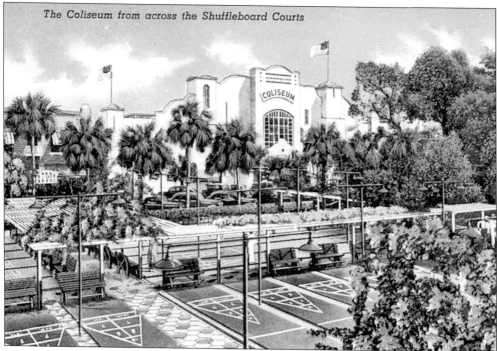

The Coliseum from across the Shuffleboard Courts

The Coliseum, which opened in 1924, was a popular dance hall during the Roaring Twenties and many of the famous bands of the swing era played here. The shuffleboard courts in the foreground were host to the world's largest shuffleboard club—8,000 members at its peak. The Coliseum/shuffleboard complex was the center of tourist activity in St. Petersburg.

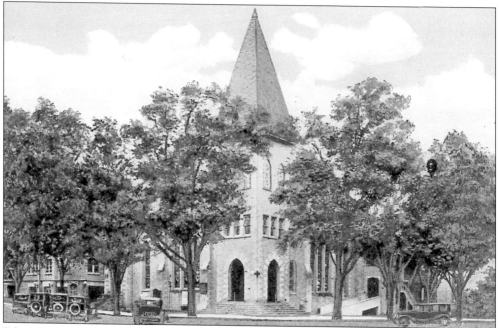

Edgar Ferdon, St. Petersburg's first professional architect, designed the stone-block First Congregational Church in 1910. The building is currently undergoing a renovation.

The boom-era Gothic revival First Methodist Church, seen here in 1924, remains a prominent part of the St. Petersburg cityscape.

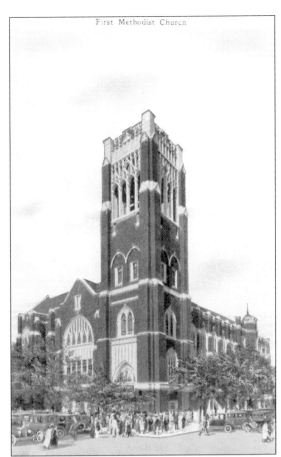

First Methodist Church

St. Petersburg's public library, now known as the Mirror Lake Library, was designed by renowned New York architect Henry Whitfield in 1915 and funded under the Carnegie system. An annex has since been added and the building has been beautifully restored.

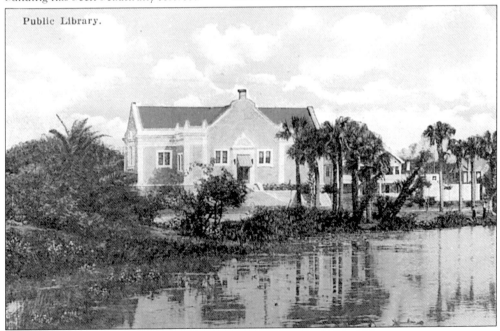

Public Library.

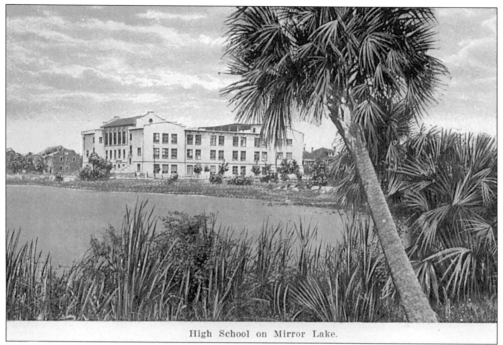

High School on Mirror Lake.

St. Petersburg High School was built in 1918 during the beginning of the boom years and was quickly outgrown. The structure was designed by William B. Ittner of St. Louis, the most famous school architect of the day. Today the building houses upscale condominiums.

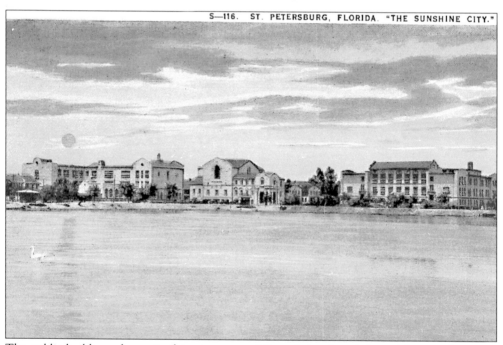

S—116. ST. PETERSBURG, FLORIDA. "THE SUNSHINE CITY."

The public buildings shown in this view across Mirror Lake, from left to right, are the junior high school (now the Adult Vocational and Education Center), the First Christian Church (now a meeting/banquet hall), and St. Petersburg High School (now condominiums).

42

Three

THE FAMOUS
GREEN BENCHES

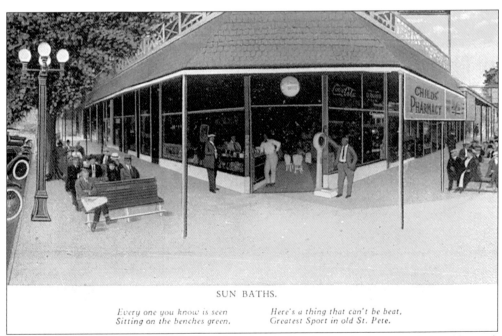

SUN BATHS.

Every one you know is seen   *Here's a thing that can't be beat,*
Sitting on the benches green.   *Greatest Sport in old St. Pete.*

The green benches, a symbol of St. Petersburg hospitality during the boom period and beyond, were conceived in 1907 by real estate magnate Noel Mitchell as a way to draw patrons to his offices at this "out of the way" corner of Fourth and Central. This corner was to become St. Petersburg's busiest and most famous, the site of the landmark Snell Arcade.

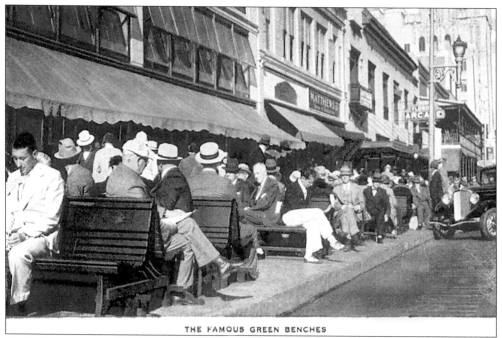

THE FAMOUS GREEN BENCHES

Mitchell's success with the benches motivated other merchants to follow suit. Soon benches multiplied throughout the city.

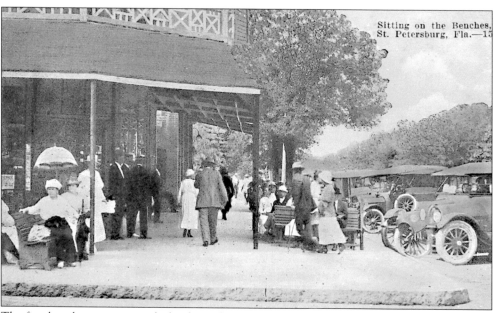

Sitting on the Benches, St. Petersburg, Fla.—1?

The first benches were painted a haphazard assortment of colors. It was up to Mayor Al Lang, in 1916, to sponsor an ordinance that all benches would be a standard size and painted green.

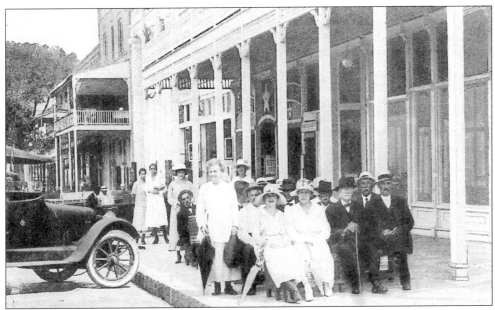

St. Petersburg became known nationwide as the "City of Green Benches" in the 1920s and 1930s. In this image, the benches are touted as St. Pete's "Favorite Outdoor Pastime."

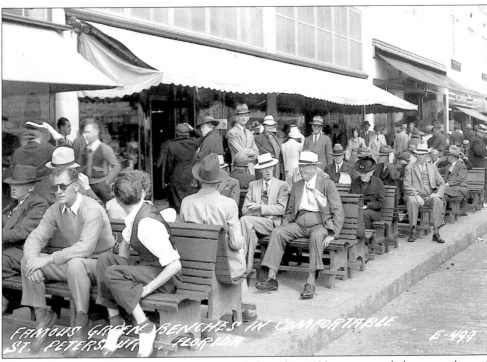

The benches along Central Avenue are crowded in this 1930s scene, and there is a line of people waiting to sit.

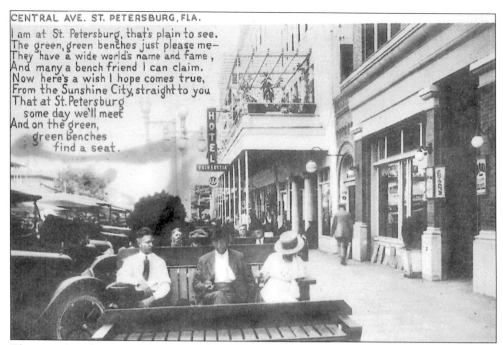

The green benches soon became world famous, immortalized in prose and verse, as a symbol of St. Petersburg's hospitality.

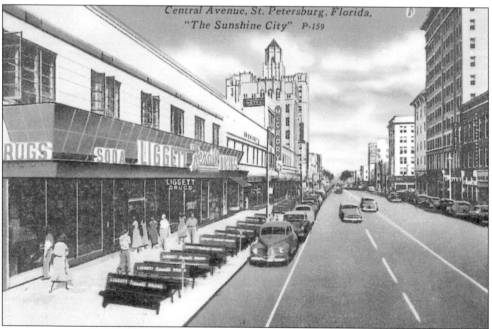

Noel Mitchell, the originator of the benches, recognized the power of advertising and his benches were marked with messages promoting his real estate business. Soon other merchants began putting advertising messages on their benches, like these in front of Liggett Rexall Drugs.

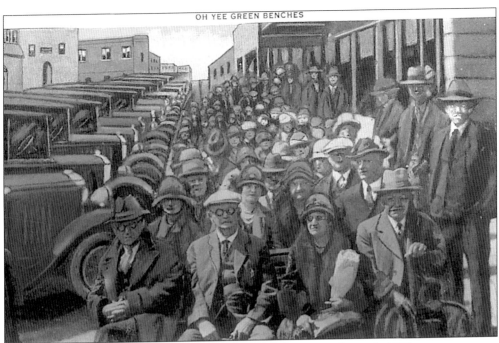

The benches are overflowing, with crowds waiting for a seat, in this early 1920s scene.

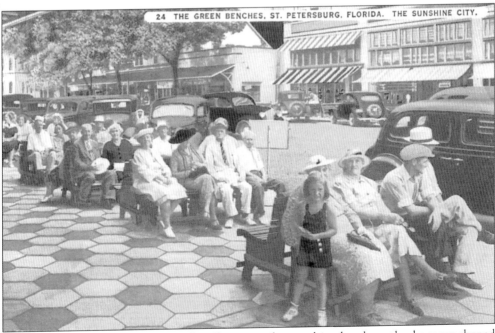

24 THE GREEN BENCHES, ST. PETERSBURG, FLORIDA. THE SUNSHINE CITY.

The "pavers" in St. Petersburg's sidewalks were often multi-colored, as the hexagon-shaped stones were replaced as needed with fashionable colors of the day.

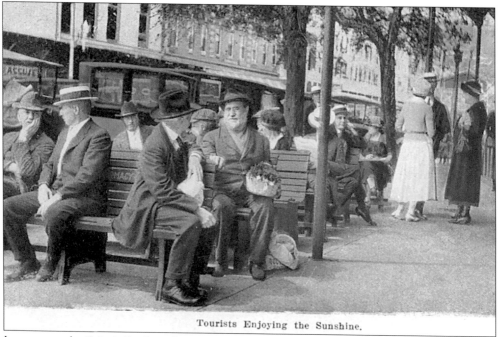

Tourists Enjoying the Sunshine.

It appears to be "Men's Day" on the green benches in this photo.

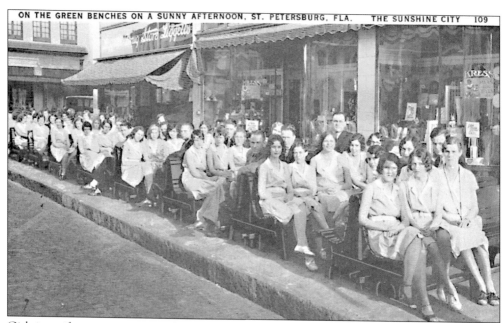

Girls in uniform enjoy a sit outside Kress's dime store on Central Avenue. The Kress chain always erected high-quality, well-constructed buildings, and this one is still a prominent landmark between Fourth and Fifth Streets.

48

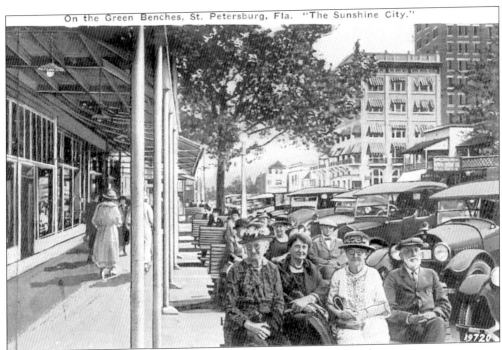

This view shows the benches and covered sidewalks of early St. Petersburg.

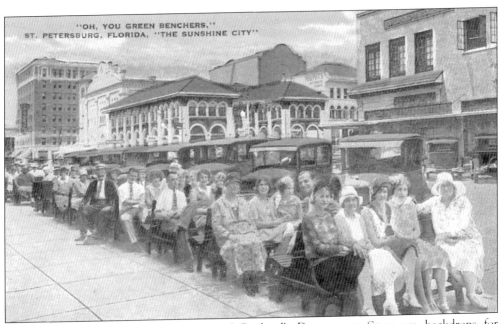

"OH, YOU GREEN BENCHERS,"
ST. PETERSBURG, FLORIDA, "THE SUNSHINE CITY"

The Plaza Theater complex, center, and Rutland's Department Store are backdrops for this scene.

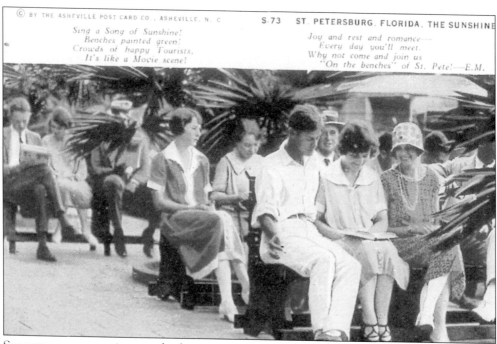

S-73   ST. PETERSBURG, FLORIDA, THE SUNSHINE

Sing a Song of Sunshine!
Benches painted green!
Crowds of happy Tourists,
It's like a Movie scene!

Joy and rest and romance—
Every day you'll meet,
Why not come and join us
"On the benches" of St. Pete!—E.M.

Sonnets were even written to the famous green benches.

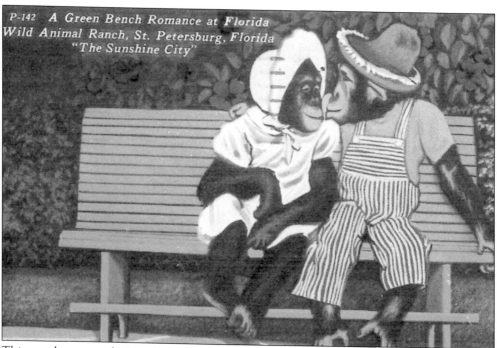

P-142   *A Green Bench Romance at Florida Wild Animal Ranch, St. Petersburg, Florida "The Sunshine City"*

This couple was caught "monkeying" around on a secluded bench!

50

Four

TOURIST ACCOMMODATIONS

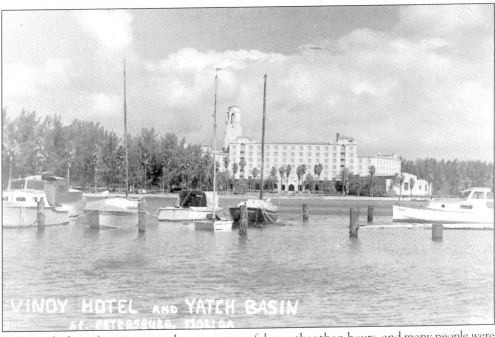

VINOY HOTEL AND YATCH BASIN
ST. PETERSBURG, FLORIDA

In the early days of tourism, travel was a matter of days rather than hours, and many people were reluctant to leave the comforts of home for an arduous journey and uncertain accommodations upon arrival. But a barrage of promotion and the promise of sunshine brought the tourists to St. Petersburg. The city rose to the occasion, offering fine accommodations ranging from grand hotels for the wealthy—such as the Vinoy, pictured here—to tourist courts and guesthouses for the less affluent.

51

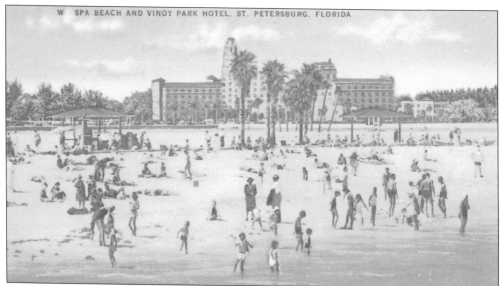

Designed by renowned architect Henry L. Taylor at a cost of $3.5 million, the opulent Vinoy opened to much fanfare on January 1, 1926. The hotel was used as army barracks during World War II and was closed in 1974. It was restored to its former glory in the 1980s—at a cost of $93 million—and is now the four-star Vinoy Renaissance.

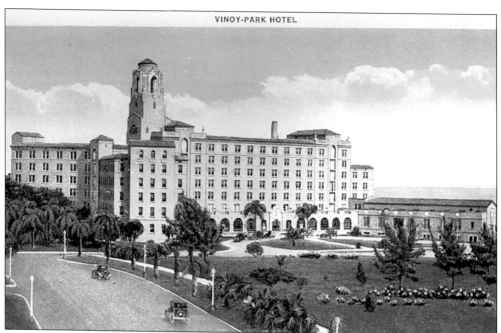

VINOY-PARK HOTEL

The Vinoy is one of three Grand Hotels in the area that have been restored and are still being operated in the Grand style. The others are the Don CeSar at St. Petersburg Beach and the Belleview Biltmore near Clearwater. Two other Grand hotels, the Rolyat and Tampa Bay Hotels, have also been restored and are being used as educational facilities.

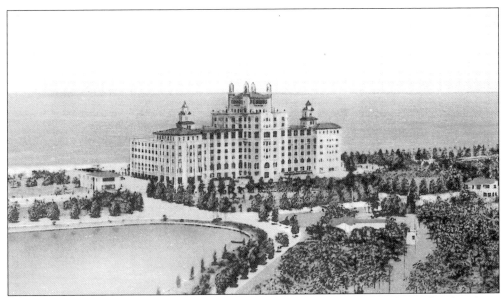

The magnificent Don CeSar has presided over St. Pete Beach since 1927. The opulent hotel was constructed over a three-year period by Massachusetts native Thomas J. Rowe at a cost of $1.4 million. It was named after Don CeSar de Bazan, the principal character in the opera *Maritana*. Like the Vinoy, the hotel was used by the military during World War II. It was restored in the 1970s to the beautiful Pink Lady of today.

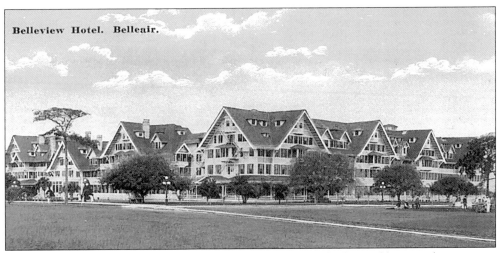

The Belleview Hotel in Belleair was the area's first Grand Hotel. The rambling wooden structure was constructed in 1888 by railroad magnate Henry B. Plant and was part of the Plant system of hotels built along the west coast of Florida to rival Henry Flagler's magnificent Grand Hotels on the East Coast. The Belleview has been continually operated as a first-class hostelry since its founding.

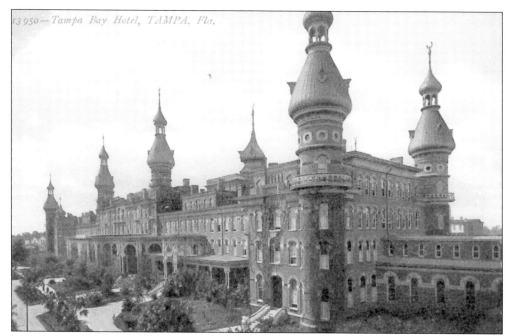

The mammoth Moorish-style Tampa Bay Hotel opened in February 1891 as the second Plant system hotel in the Tampa Bay area. It was described when it opened as "one of the modern wonders of the world."

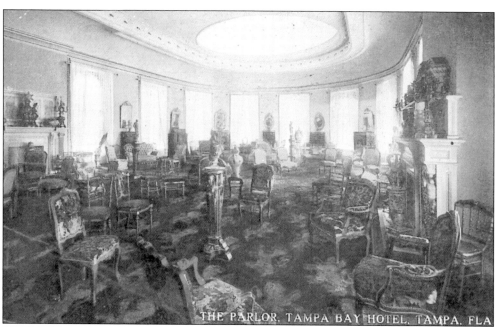

THE PARLOR, TAMPA BAY HOTEL, TAMPA, FLA

The lavishly appointed parlor is typical of the "no expense spared" approach Plant took in building and furnishing the hotel. It proved, in fact, too costly to maintain and, in 1927, closed its doors. In 1933 the building reopened as the University of Tampa, which it remains today.

The Rolyat was the pride and joy of high rolling I.M. "Handsome Jack" Taylor. Taylor's developments spared no expense in their lavishness, and the Rolyat ("Taylor" spelled backwards) was no exception. Famed architect Henry Taylor (no relation), who also did the grand Vinoy and Jungle Hotels, designed the hotel. This scene shows a terracotta wishing well on the Rolyat grounds.

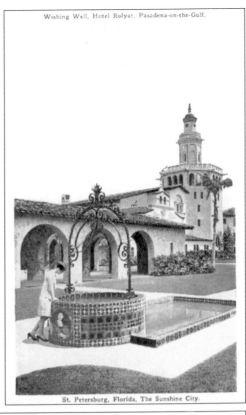

Wishing Well, Hotel Rolyat, Pasadena-on-the-Gulf.

St. Petersburg, Florida. The Sunshine City.

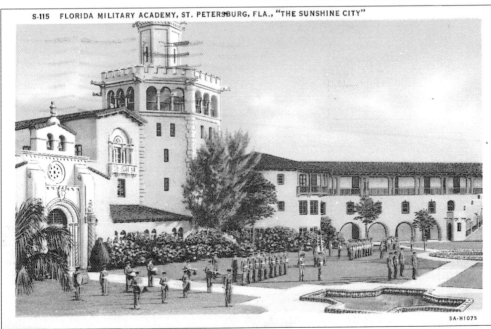

S-115   FLORIDA MILITARY ACADEMY, ST. PETERSBURG, FLA., "THE SUNSHINE CITY"

The Rolyat proved too expensive to be profitable and was purchased by the Florida Military Academy in 1929. The building, in Pasadena, is now home to Stetson University College of Law.

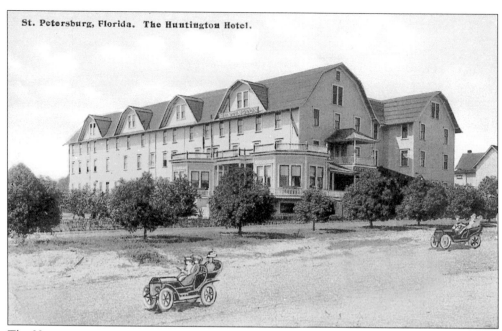

The Huntington was constructed during the 1890s and became one of St. Petersburg's leading hotels. This early view dates to 1910.

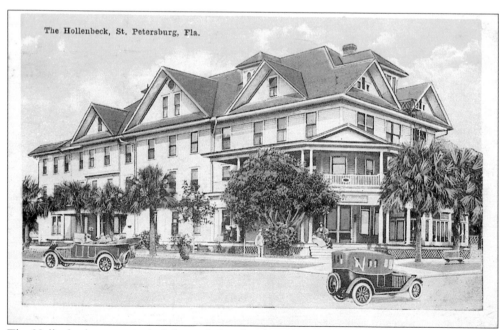

The Hollenbeck was typical of the early hotel style with wooden decoration and gables. It was later known as the Beverly Hotel.

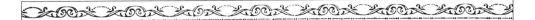

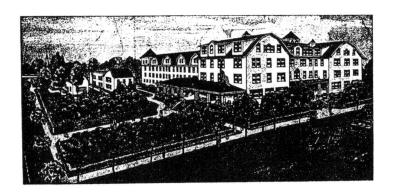

Hotel Huntington

A MODERN American Plan hotel, operated in the exclusive residential section 'mid a small orange and grapefruit grove overlooking Tampa Bay. The Huntington is within a stone's throw of all outdoor sports, theatres and churches, and is one of the chief centers of winter social activities. Write for booklet.

MUSIC DAILY

J. LEE BARNES, Prop.   PAUL BARNES, Mgr.

ST. PETERSBURG, FLORIDA

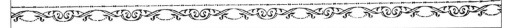

The Huntington was described as being "in an exclusive residential section amid a small orange and grapefruit grove" in this 1926 advertisement.

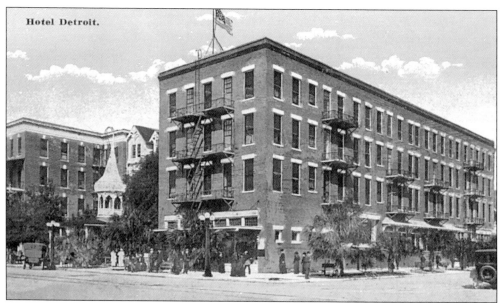

Hotel Detroit.

One of St. Petersburg's earliest hotels, the Detroit was constructed in 1888. It is shown as it appeared during the boom era (and today) after being substantially enlarged in 1924. The Detroit is currently being renovated into luxury apartments.

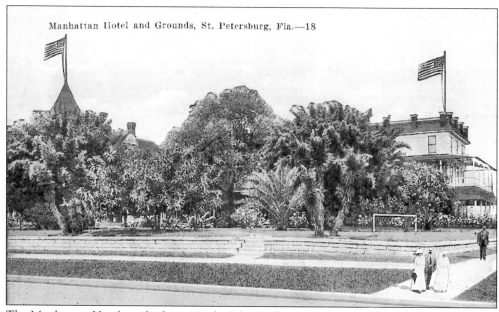

Manhattan Hotel and Grounds, St. Petersburg, Fla.—18

The Manhattan Hotel was built in 1891 by John Williams, a co-founder of St. Petersburg, as his residence. It became a hotel after being enlarged in 1912.

It's June on the Hotel Detroit Veranda

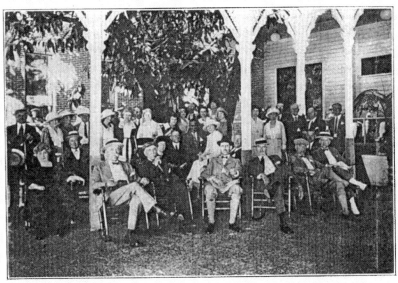

Underwood & Un'er ood

People who visit St. Petersburg are mostly on pleasure bent. It is safe to assume that most of them in their selection of a hotel would prefer one where the environment assures comfort, pleasure, rest, congeniality and, above all, **service.**

The Hotel Detroit embodies all the features recognized as essential to the desires of the traaeler.

The refined informality of its social activities makes a distinct appeal to red-blooded folk.

The Detroit is one of the most distinctive of American Hotels and is famed far and wide for its general service and its genuine hospitality. It is always June on the wonderful veranda of the Detroit Hotel. **36 hours from zero to 70 in the shade.**

HOTEL DETROIT

St. Petersburg, Florida

FRANK FORTUNE PULVER, Owner   BAINBRIDGE HAYWARD, Manager

St. Petersburg's hotels were heavily promoted during the boom period, and this ad, which appeared in the *Tourist News* edited by Karl Grismer, is no exception.

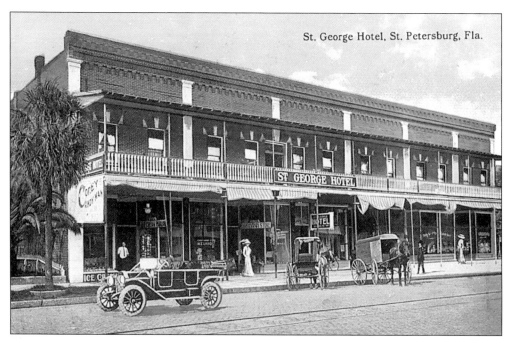

The St. George Hotel, shown nearly a century ago, was located on Central Avenue.

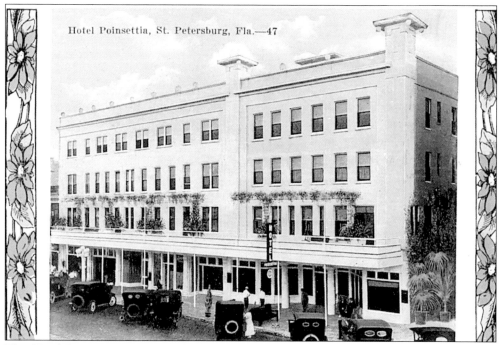

The Hotel Poinsettia, constructed prior to the boom, catered to traveling salesmen. It was substantially enlarged in 1924 to accommodate the tourist influx.

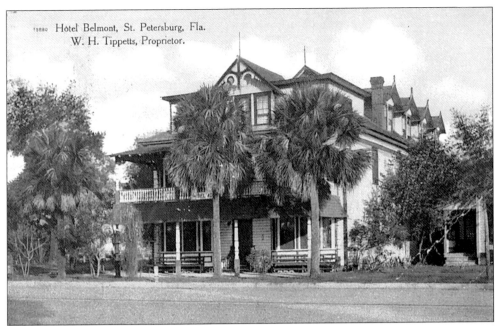

The Hotel Belmont was originally built in 1893 as the Sixth Avenue House. It was purchased and renovated by William H. Tippetts in 1902. The gabled style was typical of late-1800s hotel construction.

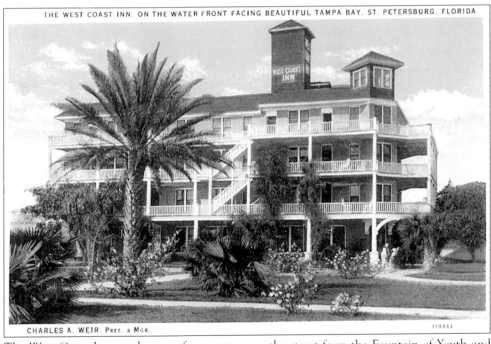

The West Coast Inn on the waterfront was across the street from the Fountain of Youth and was popular with health enthusiasts. The message on this 1930 card refers to "flowers and palms everywhere." The hotel was demolished in 1967.

Built in 1926, the Pennsylvania was the last of the seasonal hotels that were open only during the winter tourist season. It is currently being restored.

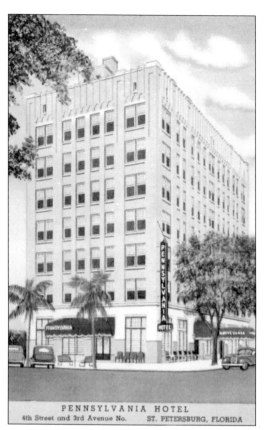

PENNSYLVANIA HOTEL
4th Street and 3rd Avenue No.   ST. PETERSBURG, FLORIDA

The Ponce de Leon, completed in 1922, was built during the city's hotel construction boom in the early- to mid-1920s. During the period from 1922 to 1926, eleven major hotels were completed. This hotel is currently undergoing renovation on the site at Central Avenue and First Street.

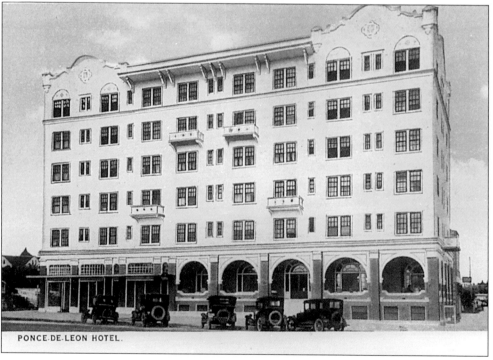

PONCE-DE-LEON HOTEL.

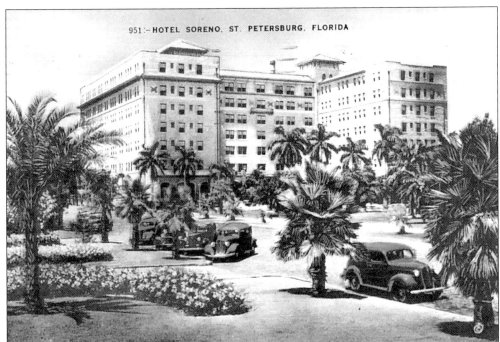

951:—HOTEL SORENO, ST. PETERSBURG, FLORIDA

The Soreno was touted as St. Petersburg's first million-dollar hotel when it opened on January 1, 1924. It was built by and named after Soren Lund, a Denmark native who came to St. Petersburg in 1910. He had previously owned the Huntington Hotel. The Soreno was demolished in a spectacular explosion for a movie scene in 1993.

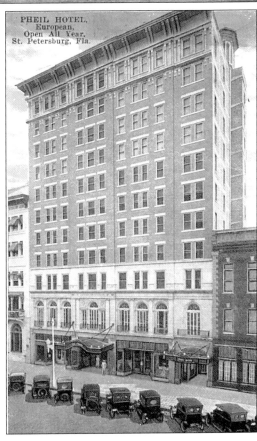

A prominent Central Avenue landmark, the Pheil was originally built as a movie theater and hotel by Abe Pheil, an early St. Petersburg mayor. A compulsive fear of fire caused Pheil to build his theater backwards, with the screen in front, so that the projector, with its flammable film, could be housed in a detached rear room safely outside the building.

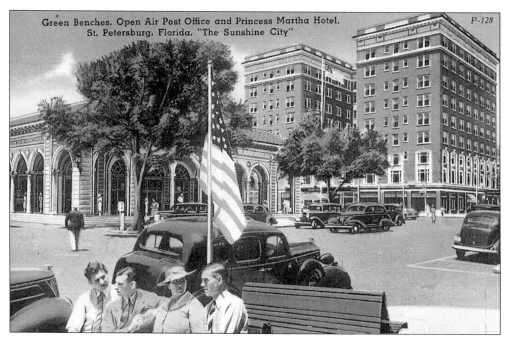

Green Benches, Open Air Post Office and Princess Martha Hotel, St. Petersburg, Florida, "The Sunshine City"

The only boom-era hotel to be built with public ownership through stock sales was the Mason. The hotel later went bankrupt and was bought by winter resident William Muir, who changed its name to the Princess Martha in honor of his wife. Originally one of the largest and most prominent hotels in St. Petersburg, the building is now a retirement home.

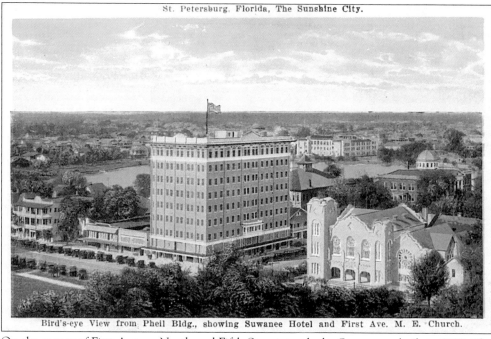

St. Petersburg, Florida, The Sunshine City.

Bird's-eye View from Pheil Bldg., showing Suwanee Hotel and First Ave. M. E. Church.

On the corner of First Avenue North and Fifth Street stands the Suwannee, built in 1923. The 200-room hotel has been renovated into offices.

Built in 1921, the Hotel Cordova was typical of the smaller facilities of the pre-boom era. It is situated opposite Williams Park and has been splendidly restored as the Pier Hotel.

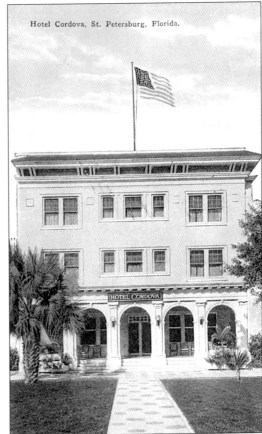

Hotel Cordova, St. Petersburg, Florida.

The Sunset Hotel was the only hotel not within walking distance of downtown when it was built at the western end of Central Avenue in 1915. Tourists lacking automobiles could ride St. Petersburg's excellent trolley system to town. Located at Park and Central, the hotel is currently being operated as the Crystal Bay Hotel.

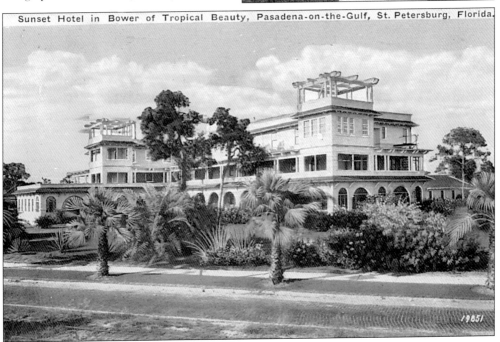

Sunset Hotel in Bower of Tropical Beauty, Pasadena-on-the-Gulf, St. Petersburg, Florida.

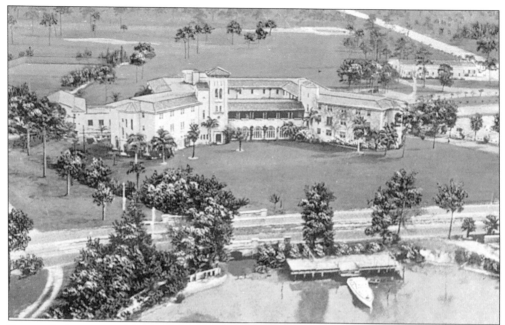

Some of the more elaborate developments combined lavish hotel accommodations and recreation in one self-contained facility. The Jungle Hotel and Country Club offered a variety of sport, social, and recreational activities, all on the premises. Henry Taylor, who also did the Vinoy, designed the Jungle Country Club.

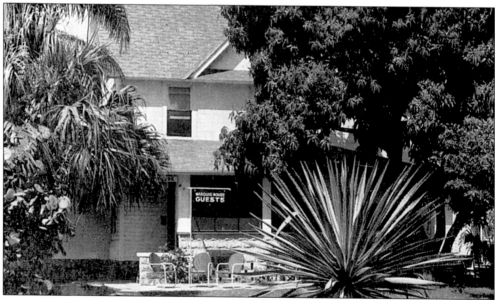

Not everyone could afford the lavish or even large hotels of the day. Tourists of more modest means were offered a variety of choices ranging from the homier guesthouses, which were the forerunners of today's bed and breakfasts, to the tourist courts, cottages, and trailer parks. A typical guesthouse of the period was the Marquis House, located on Sixth Avenue "in the rear of a 200 ft. lot away from traffic opposite Aunt Hattie's Restaurant" and "within walking distance of downtown."

American Plan - - - Ninety-three Outside Rooms - - - Private Baths - - - Sun Gardens

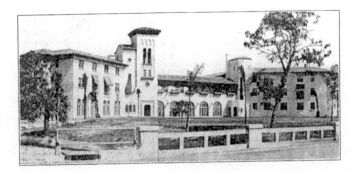

Every Facility for Resort Hotel Enjoyment *is here!*

Whatever the recreation you prefer, you'll find it easily accessible at the Jungle Hotel and Country Club. Social events vie with outdoor sports in an endless round of activities for hotel guests.

Do you like golf? There's an eighteen hole course just a step from the hotel, and a competent pro and his assistant to help you with your game.

If you like to ride, the Jungle Stables are nearby. Twenty-five Kentucky thoroughbreds are available including three and five gaited horses, jumpers, polo ponies—some gentle and some high spirited—you'll find the horse you'll want to ride among them.

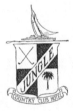

Just back of the hotel are concrete tennis courts. And across the road lies the Gulf with its many recreational opportunities.

At night—spend a quiet evening in the hotel lounge or relax in the patio. For an evening of gaiety a supper club under hotel management is closeby.

Whatever you like in sports is here, as is every social opportunity. *Rates and booklet on request.*

SPORTS

Golf—Riding—Tennis—Swimming—Fishing—Dancing—Boating
Canoeing—Trap Shooting—Private Garages—Grill

Jungle Hotel & Country Club

JOHN F. HYNES, Managing Director

ST. PETERSBURG

CAPT. J. S. SHALLCROSS
Riding Instructor

ERNEST R. ANDERSON
Golf Pro.

EDDIE BROWN
Assistant

CAPT. J. S. CRAWFORD
Riding Master

MISS MARY BRYNE GILTNER
Riding Hostess

CHAS. HYNES
Ass't Hotel Manager

CAPT. J. L. TRUESDALE
Fishing Cruisers

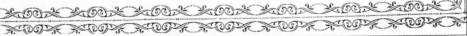

This period advertisement touts the Jungle as an early version of today's "all-inclusive resort."

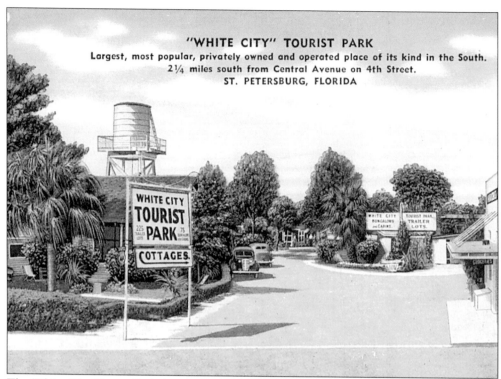

"WHITE CITY" TOURIST PARK
Largest, most popular, privately owned and operated place of its kind in the South.
2¼ miles south from Central Avenue on 4th Street.
ST. PETERSBURG, FLORIDA

The White City Tourist Park featured 225 trailer lots, 75 bungalows and cabins, a clubhouse, a recreation hall, a dance hall, and shuffleboard and horseshoe courts in a 12-acre park.

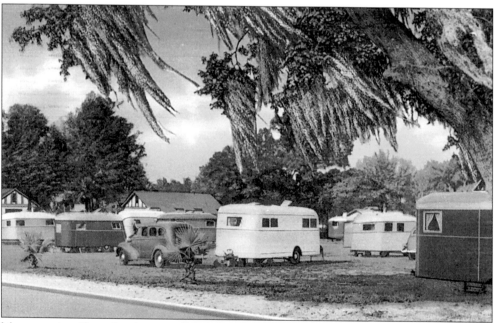

Many tourists "brought their own" lodging and took space in local trailer parks. The less prosperous of these were sometimes referred to as "Tin Can Tourists," as they often ate meals straight from the can.

Five

PARKS, GARDENS, AND ATTRACTIONS

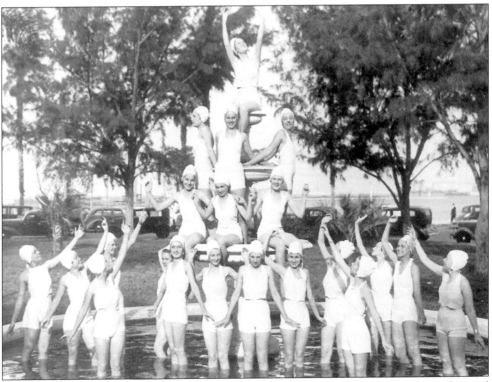

This photograph of girls posing on a fountain at the waterfront was taken as a publicity shot and used on a calendar promoting St. Petersburg.

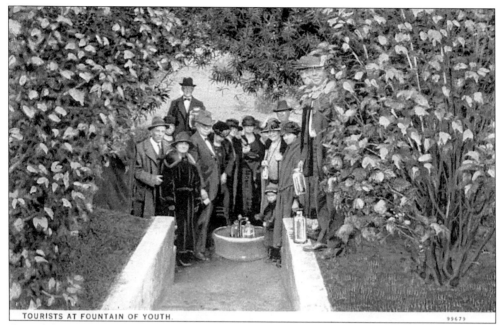

One of the major attractions the Sunshine City offered was the beautiful parks and foliage made possible by the balmy climate. St. Petersburg even had its own "Fountain of Youth" at the foot of Fourth Avenue South. A drinking fountain was added later so visitors could drop by for a pick-me-up. It was later discovered that the artesian waters contained lithium.

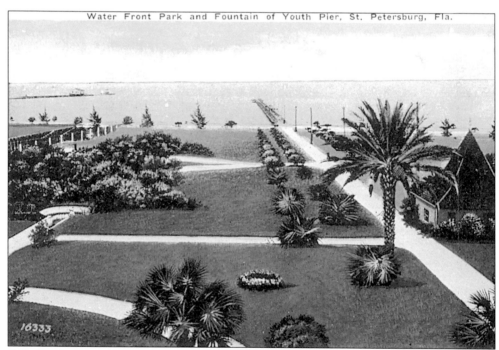

Water Front Park and Fountain of Youth Pier, St. Petersburg, Fla.

E.H. Tomlinson, who had the artesian well drilled that supplied the Fountain of Youth, also built the Fountain of Youth Pier out into Tampa Bay. The fountain, which still exists on the edge of the Bayfront Center parking lot, can be seen on the left.

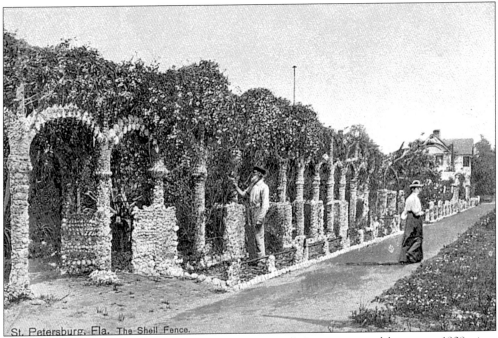

Another curiosity of early St. Petersburg was the Shell Fence, pictured here in a 1909 view. Hundreds of thousands of shells were collected from the Gulf to build this fence at the home of Owen Albright on First Street North at Second Avenue.

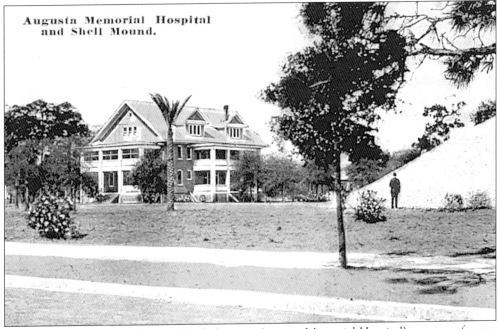

Augusta Memorial Hospital and Shell Mound.

The Shell Mound at Shell Mound Park (next to Augusta Memorial Hospital) was one of seven regional mounds that bore testament to an early Indian civilization. Unfortunately the others were destroyed for use as road fill, and this mound also eventually succumbed to hospital expansion plans.

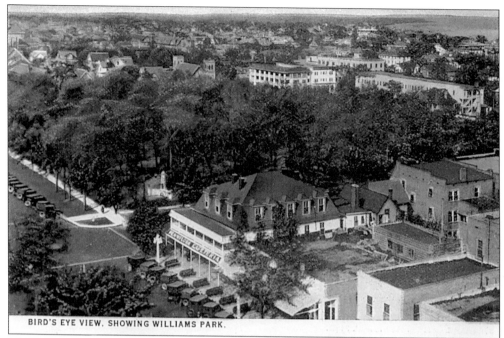

BIRD'S EYE VIEW, SHOWING WILLIAMS PARK.

This view gives a bird's-eye look at Williams Park and the surrounding hotels and churches, with Tampa Bay in the distance. The Pennflora Cafeteria in the foreground was one of many cafeterias that were popular until the end of World War II.

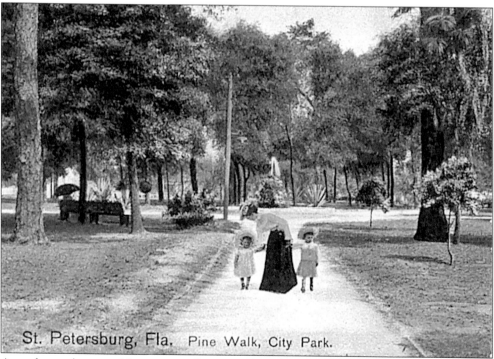

St. Petersburg, Fla. Pine Walk, City Park.

A mother and young girls enjoy a walk among the palms and pines at City Park, c. 1907. City Park later became Williams Park in honor of John C. Williams, a founder of St. Petersburg.

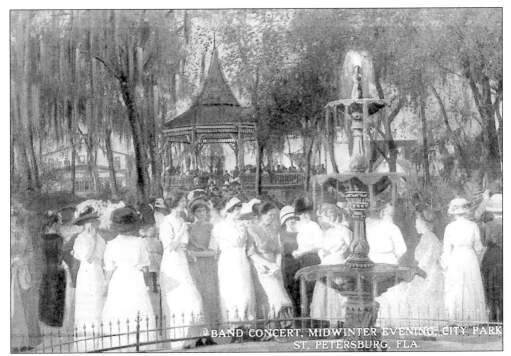

BAND CONCERT, MIDWINTER EVENING, CITY PARK
ST. PETERSBURG, FLA.

Ladies in their finery congregate at the fountain in City Park, c. 1913, to enjoy a mid-winter evening band concert.

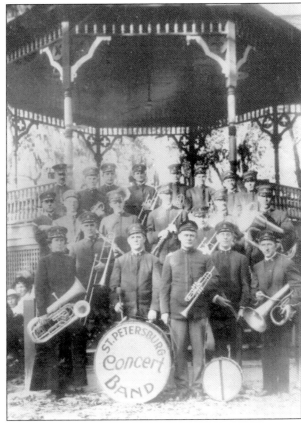

The St. Petersburg Concert Band, shown here under the gazebo at Williams Park, was founded in 1894 by T.A. Whitted and A.C. Pheil. Band concerts remained a very popular form of entertainment at the park throughout the boom era and continue to this day.

73

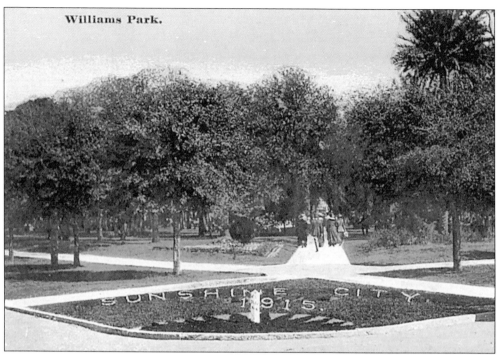

Williams Park.

This scene above at Williams Park includes a flower garden that spells out the words "Sunshine City 1915."

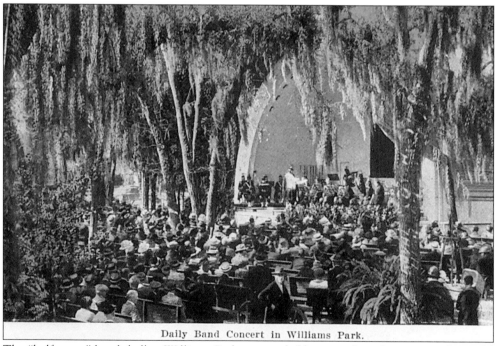

Daily Band Concert in Williams Park.

The "half moon" band shell at Williams Park surrounded by moss-draped trees was a beautiful setting for the daily concerts held during the winter season. A later version of the band shell, which is still in use today, has a modern peaked roof.

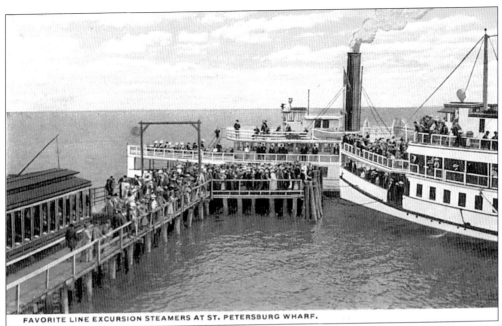

FAVORITE LINE EXCURSION STEAMERS AT ST. PETERSBURG WHARF.

Here two Favorite Line steamers discharge a hoard of excursionists to waiting streetcars at the Electric Pier. The Favorite Line was established by F.A. Davis in 1905 with his purchase of the 400-passenger steamboat *Favorite*. Davis, who also brought electricity to the city, built the Electric Pier to have a place for his steamboat to land.

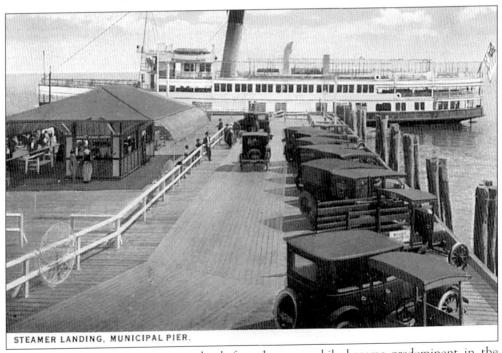

STEAMER LANDING, MUNICIPAL PIER.

Steamboat transportation was popular before the automobile became predominant in the mid-1920s. A steamer landing was at the foot of Municipal Pier before the construction of the Million-Dollar Pier and Casino.

75

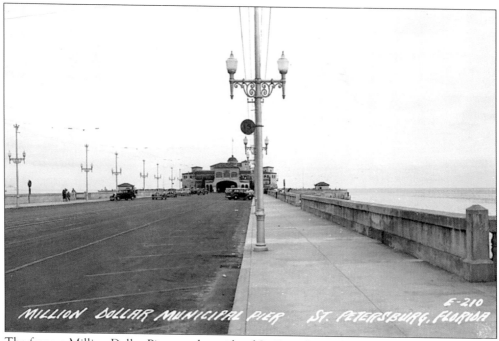

The famous Million-Dollar Pier was the pride of St. Petersburg when it was completed in 1926. The city's most popular recreation spot, it was usually jammed with visitors. The pier featured bright electric streetlights and ample parking leading up to (and around) the famous casino.

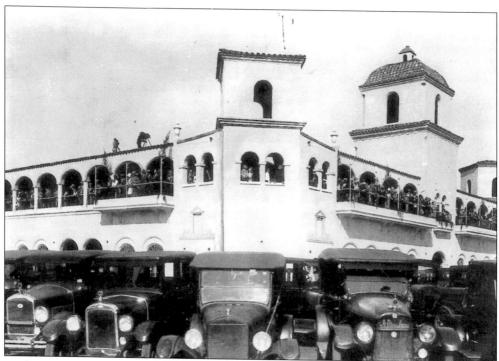

In this photograph, crowds line the balconies and autos jam the parking spaces during the season at the pier.

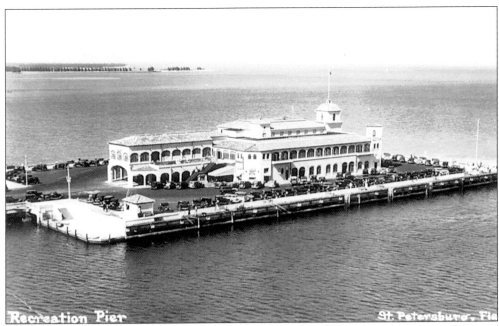

Called the Recreation Pier in early days, the waterfront complex was a magnet for tourists, and boasted a beach, solarium, fishing pier, and open-air ballroom.

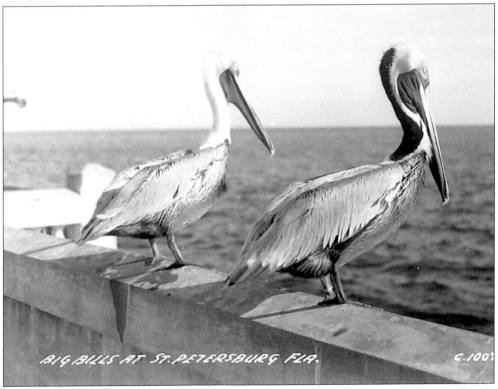

The pelican, with its huge beak ready for a tourist-fed meal, became a symbol of early St. Petersburg.

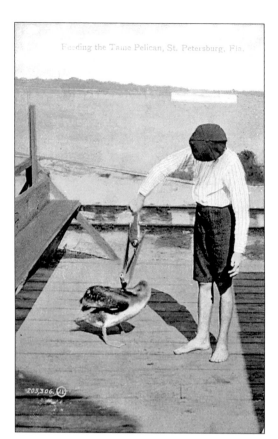

Feeding the Tame Pelican, St. Petersburg, Fla.

203306

In this photograph, an early "casual dresser" accommodates a hungry pelican.

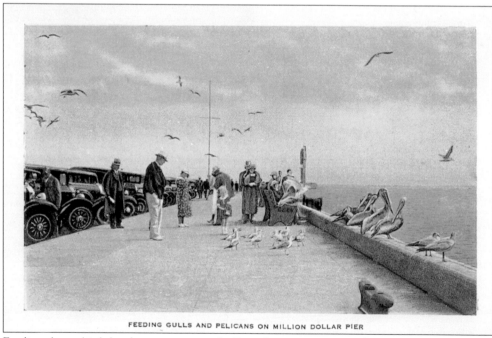

FEEDING GULLS AND PELICANS ON MILLION DOLLAR PIER

Feeding the seabirds has been a common St. Petersburg pastime over the decades.

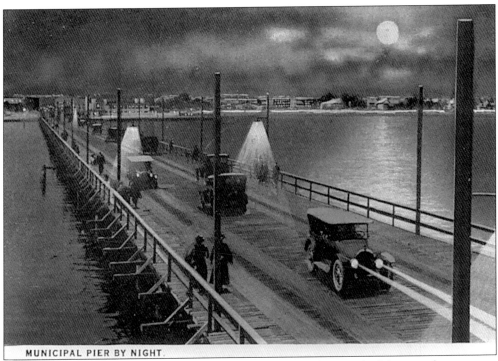

MUNICIPAL PIER BY NIGHT.

The early Municipal Pier is shown "by night" in this obviously retouched daytime shot.

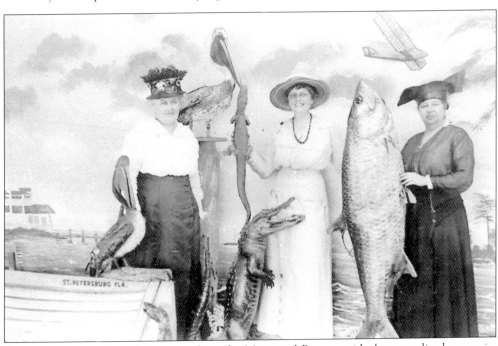

Comic portraits such as this one made at the Municipal Pier were ideal personalized souvenirs to send home. The woman in the middle is Mary Wheeler Eaton, the founder of the St. Petersburg Historical Society. She was co-owner, with her husband, William, of Eaton's Groves.

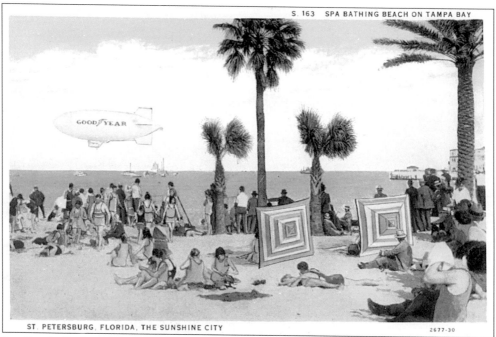

GOODYEAR

ST. PETERSBURG, FLORIDA, THE SUNSHINE CITY   2677-30

Spa Beach, St. Petersburg's "downtown beach" on Tampa Bay, was popular during the boom era with tourists leery of the "mosquito and palmetto-infested" Gulf shore. This view includes the Goodyear Blimp, probably quite a novelty in the age of steamboats and railroads.

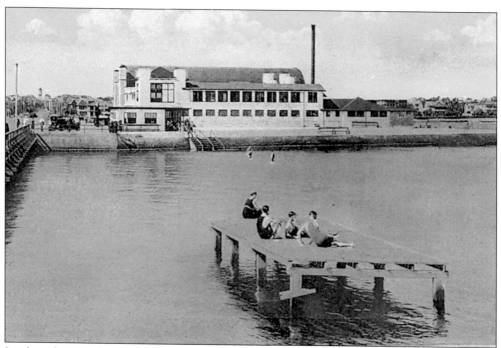

In this photograph, swimmers enjoy a rest on this diving platform at Spa Beach. In the background is the Bath House and downtown St. Petersburg. Spa Beach remains a downtown landmark beside the pier.

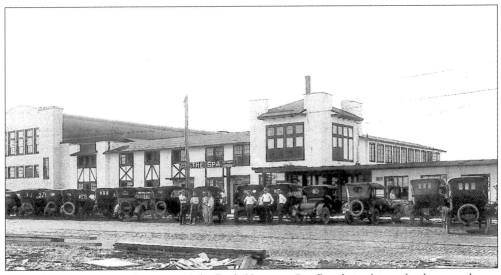

All parking spaces are taken around the Bath House at Spa Beach in this early photograph.

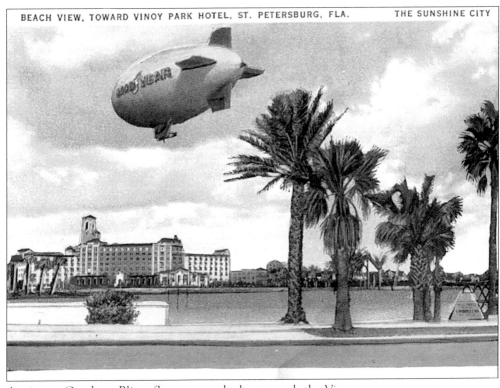

BEACH VIEW, TOWARD VINOY PARK HOTEL, ST. PETERSBURG, FLA.   THE SUNSHINE CITY

A vintage Goodyear Blimp floats across the bay towards the Vinoy.

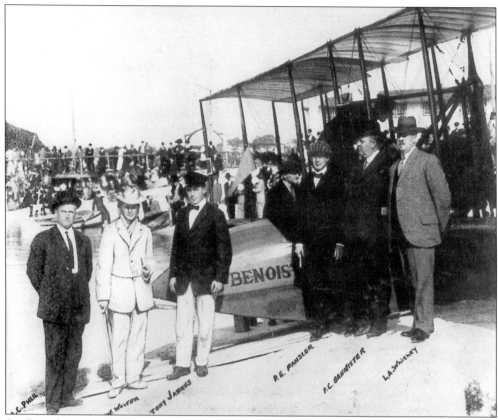

St. Petersburg was the site of the world's first scheduled commercial airline, the Benoist bi-plane, which was piloted by Tony Jannus (third from left). The prominent St. Petersburg citizens shown here were responsible for the formation of the airline, which flew between St. Petersburg and Tampa. The airline began service on January 1, 1912.

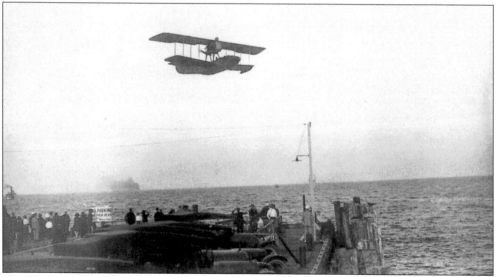

A crowd watches the Benoist in flight from Municipal Pier in this photograph.

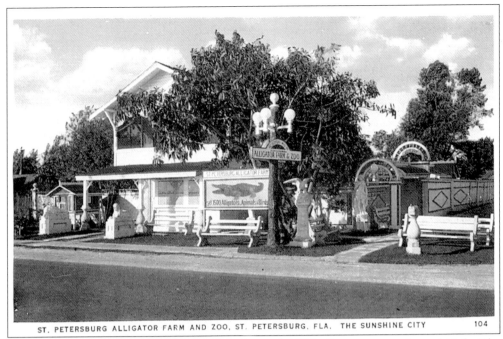

The St. Petersburg Alligator Farm and Zoo boasted 1,500 alligators, animals, and birds. The prime attraction was, of course, the gators.

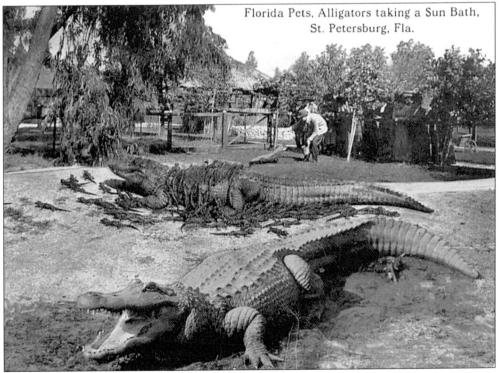

Tourists' fascination with the alligator was evident in the proliferation of postcards depicting "smiling" alligators.

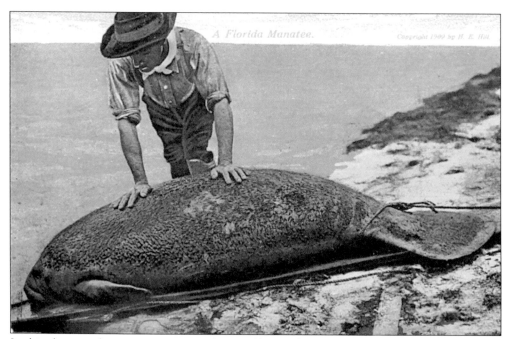

In this photograph, a manatee, now endangered but at the time merely another "fish," is caught and examined.

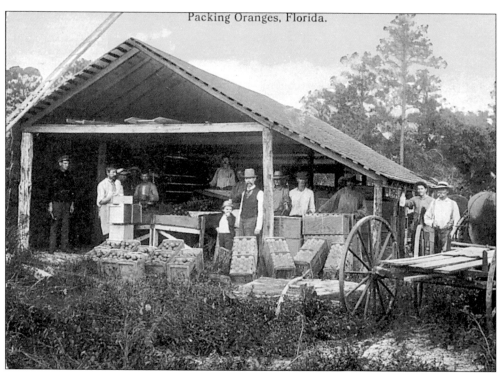

Tropical fruits, especially citrus, were shipped north by early entrepreneurs, piquing interest in Florida and the Sunshine City among would-be tourists.

A stylish, Roaring Twenties "flapper" is pictured among a cluster of Florida oranges.

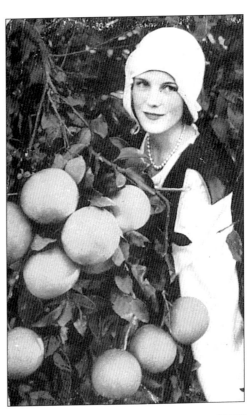

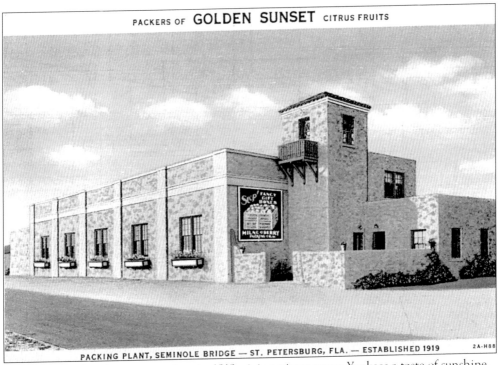

PACKERS OF **GOLDEN SUNSET** CITRUS FRUITS

PACKING PLANT, SEMINOLE BRIDGE — ST. PETERSBURG, FLA. — ESTABLISHED 1919   2A-H88

This packing plant began operations in 1919, giving winter-weary Yankees a taste of sunshine.

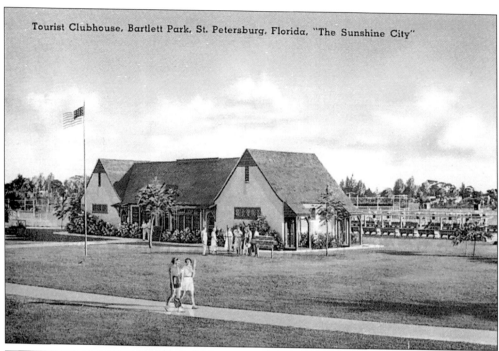

Tourist Clubhouse, Bartlett Park, St. Petersburg, Florida, "The Sunshine City"

Bartlett Park, named in honor of civic leader and educator A.F. Bartlett, was one of St. Petersburg's first Works Projects Administration programs during the Depression.

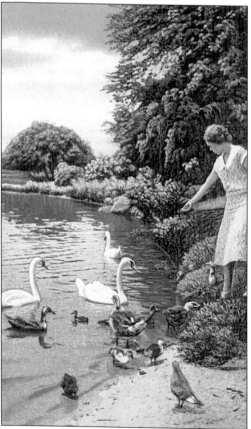

Area lakes were popular spots for feeding the numerous waterfowl that wintered in the area along with the "snowbirds."

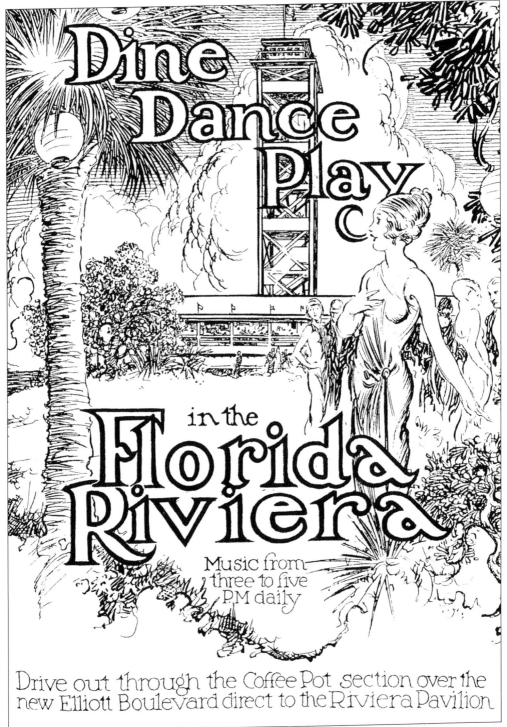

Dine Dance Play

in the Florida Riviera

Music from three to five PM daily

Drive out through the Coffee Pot section over the new Elliott Boulevard direct to the Riviera Pavilion

Dancing pavilions and ballrooms were common in the 1920s and 1930s and were a major attraction for visitors and residents alike. This pavilion, called the Florida Riviera, was located near the fashionable Coffee Pot Bayou area.

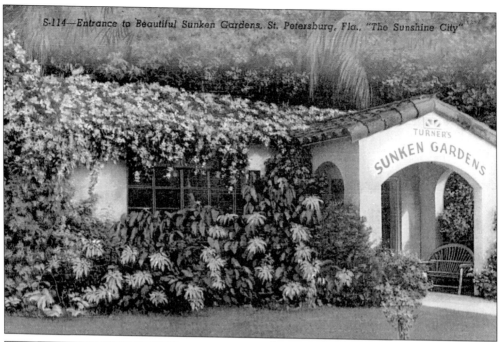

S-114—Entrance to Beautiful Sunken Gardens, St. Petersburg, Fla., "The Sunshine City"

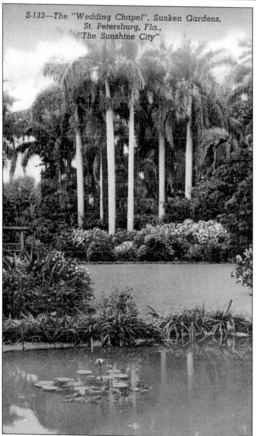

S-132—The "Wedding Chapel", Sunken Gardens, St. Petersburg, Fla., "The Sunshine City"

In 1924, Sunken Gardens was started as a small gift shop and six-acre garden by plumber George Turner Sr. It became one of the state's premiere tourist attractions by the 1930s.

Turner, whose hobby was horticulture, drained the small lake on the property, leaving the rich muck that was ideally suited for creating the lush gardens. Formal gardens added to the attractiveness of the Sunken Gardens paradise.

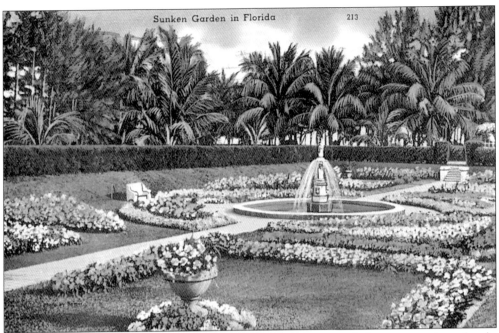

The tropical splendor of Sunken Gardens became known around the country through ads, colorful postcards, and word-of-mouth. Today, Sunken Gardens, as magnificent as ever, is owned and maintained by the City of St. Petersburg. As in the past, the gardens offer tourists and residents alike a restful, picturesque respite from everyday life.

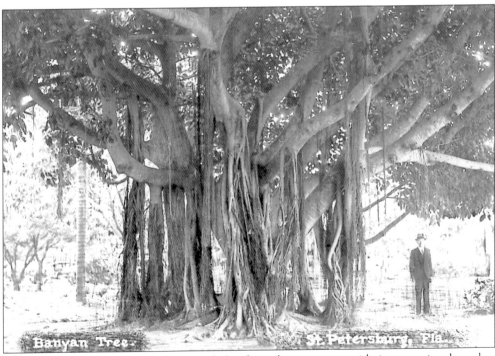

Banyan Tree.   St. Petersburg, Fla.

Victorian tourists loved curiosities, and this huge banyan tree, with its spanning branches dwarfing the man beside it, was a sight to behold and write home about.

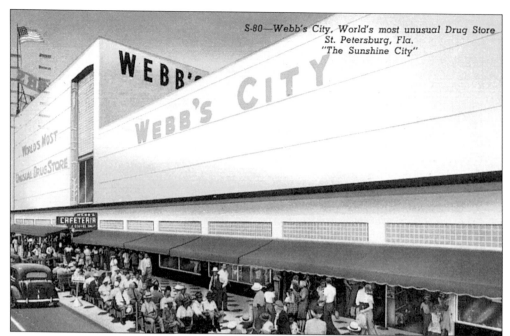

Highway billboards on routes south proclaimed St. Petersburg home of "The World's Most Unusual Drug Store." Tennessee native James Earl "Doc" Webb, a relentless promoter, founded the tiny drugstore and turned it into this mammoth wonder spanning several blocks. The prototype for today's super drug outlets, the attraction flourished until the Webb family sold out in the mid-1970s.

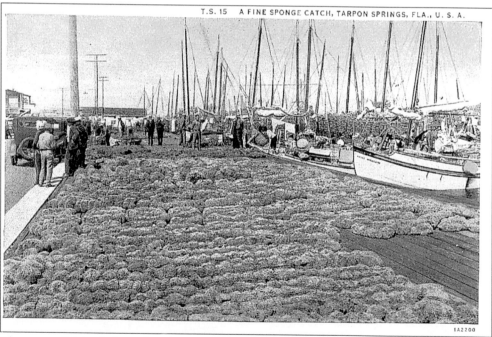

The sponge fishing industry has dominated Tarpon Springs since the early days. The "old world" charm has also been an attraction to tourists.

Six

SPORTS AND RECREATION

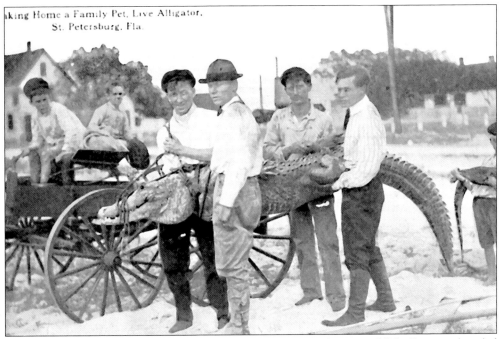

Hunting and fishing were prime attractions in a region abounding in wildlife. Facetiously titled "Taking Home a Family Pet," this card actually features the spoils of an alligator hunt.

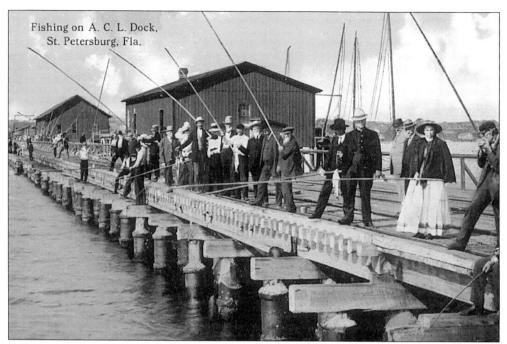

Fishing on A. C. L. Dock,
St. Petersburg, Fla.

Fish were abundant in the waters of Tampa Bay, and fishing was a big draw for early tourists. Fishermen (and woman) crowd the ACL Dock, built by the Atlantic Coast Line Railroad to connect the rail line with steamship traffic.

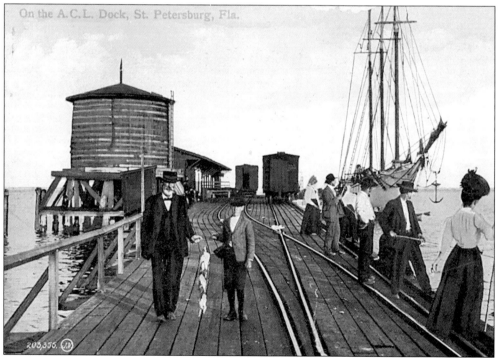

On the A.C.L. Dock, St. Petersburg, Fla.

Here, formally dressed fishers vie for space on the ACL Dock with rail lines, storage tanks, and a sloop.

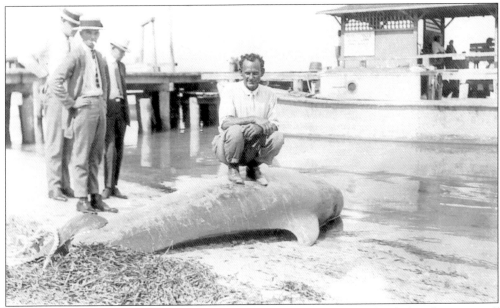

George Roberts, a famous fishing guide, is shown here atop a shark he landed in the waters off Pass-a-Grille. The story is told that the colorful Roberts skipped his wedding to fish, proclaiming, "Lady, you can get married anytime, but you have to catch these tarpon when they're hungry."

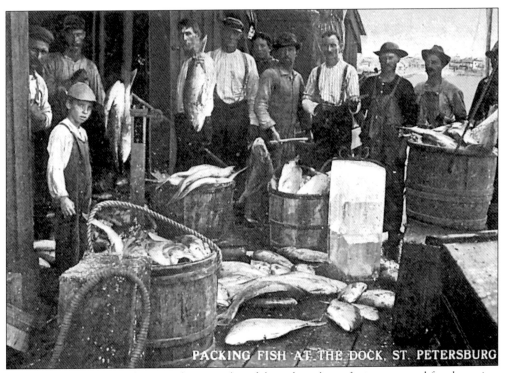

PACKING FISH AT THE DOCK, ST. PETERSBURG

This scene of fishermen bringing home a plentiful catch makes a fitting postcard for the writer who says, "I put in most of my time fishing for pleasure."

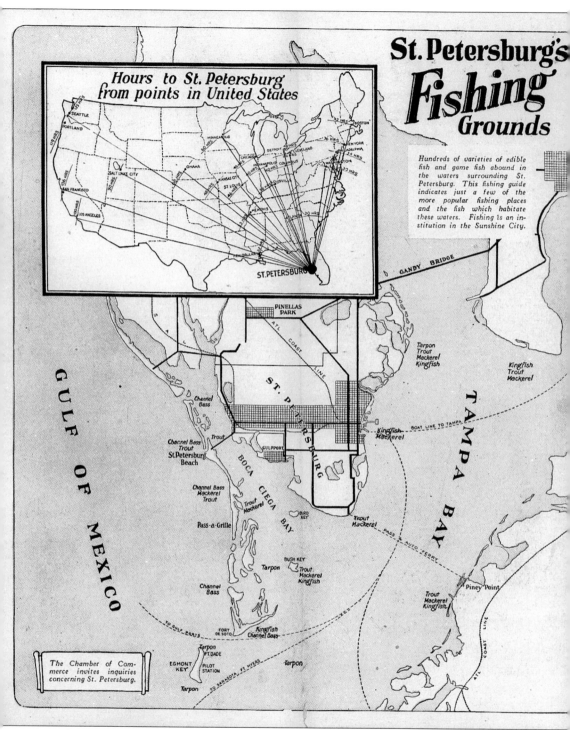

St. Petersburg's
Fishing
Grounds

Hours to St. Petersburg from points in United States

Hundreds of varieties of edible fish and game fish abound in the waters surrounding St. Petersburg. This fishing guide indicates just a few of the more popular fishing places and the fish which habitate these waters. Fishing is an institution in the Sunshine City.

GANDY BRIDGE

PINELLAS PARK

ST. PETERSBURG

GULF OF MEXICO

TAMPA BAY

BOCA CIEGA BAY

ATL. COAST LINE

Tarpon
Trout
Mackerel
Kingfish

Kingfish
Trout
Mackerel

BOAT LINE TO TAMPA

Kingfish
Mackerel

Channel Bass

Channel Bass
Trout
St. Petersburg Beach

Trout

GULFPORT

Channel Bass
Mackerel
Trout

Trout
Mackerel

BIRD KEY

Trout
Mackerel

PASS A AUTO FERRY

Pass-a-Grille

BUSH KEY

Tarpon

Trout
Mackerel
Kingfish

Trout
Mackerel
Kingfish

Piney Point

Channel Bass

FORT DE SOTO

Kingfish
Channel Bass

Tarpon
FT. DADE

EGMONT KEY

PILOT STATION

Tarpon

TO GULF PORTS

TO SARASOTA, FT. MYERS

Tarpon

ATL. COAST LINE

The Chamber of Commerce invites inquiries concerning St. Petersburg.

This map, prepared by the chamber of commerce in 1926, shows the prime fishing areas plus ferry routes and driving distances to major U.S. cities.

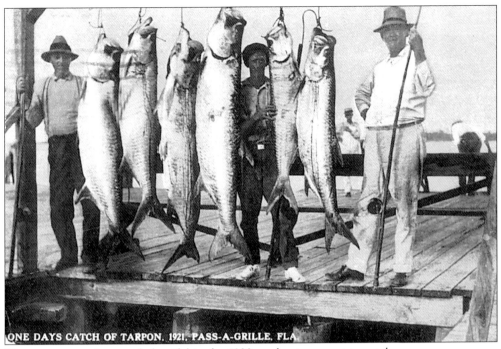

ONE DAYS CATCH OF TARPON, 1921, PASS-A-GRILLE, FLA.

The tarpon were huge and plentiful in the 1920s and quite a sport to catch.

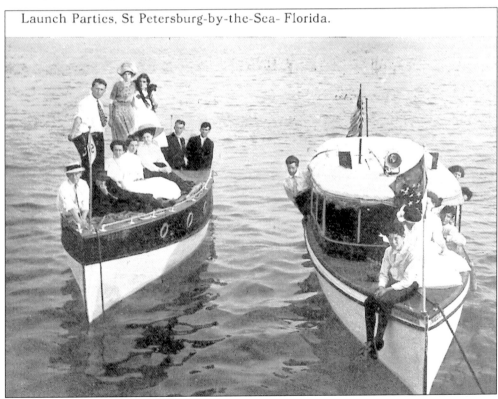

Launch Parties, St Petersburg-by-the-Sea- Florida.

In this photograph, Victorian boaters tie up at "St. Petersburg-by-the-Sea."

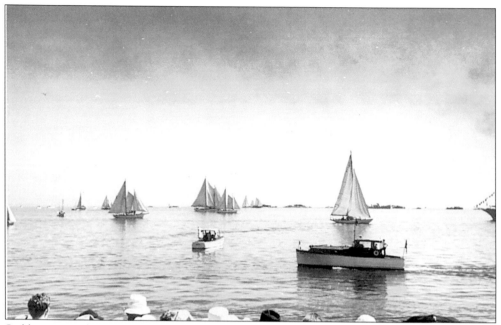

Sail boating and motor boating were popular recreational pursuits.

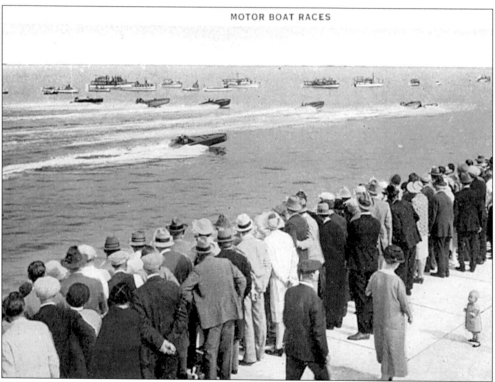

MOTOR BOAT RACES

Here, crowds line the pier to watch a speedboat race. A 1920s promotional brochure boasts, "Some of the fastest boats in Florida waters are owned by St. Petersburg power boat enthusiasts."

ENJOY THE BEAUTY OF FLORIDA — ABOARD

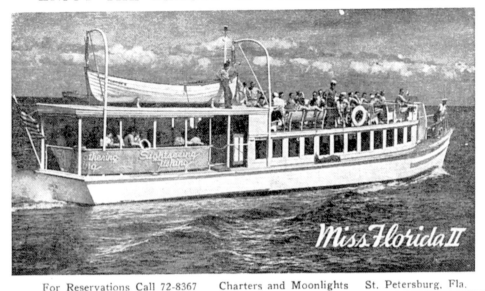

For Reservations Call 72-8367   Charters and Moonlights   St. Petersburg, Fla.

Sightseeing tours were a popular, sunny day activity. The *Miss Florida II* sailed daily from the Central Yacht Basin and toured the harbor and waterfront residential areas.

CRUISE .... ▲

ACROSS TAMPA BAY and up the tropical Little Manatee River, where many interesting sights add to the pleasure of this lovely cruise. Stop at Shell Point where Dinner will be served on the boat.

Into Bayboro Harbor where you will see the Government Reservation, also Coffee Pot Bayou where some of St. Petersburg's most beautiful homes are located.

Leaves Pier No. 41, Central Yacht Basin, at 10:30 A. M., Daily except Saturday. A double deck boat, with a comfortable cabin, clean rest room, new Diesel motor, and operating under the Dept. of Commerce Bureau of Marine and Navigation of Washington, D. C. . . . .

................................on the beautiful Miss Florida II
ST. PETERSBURG, FLORIDA

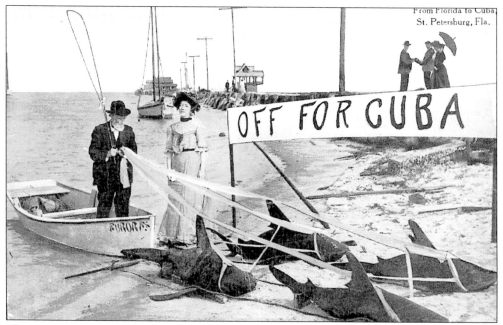

OFF FOR CUBA

This gentleman appears to be hitching up his dolphins for a rowboat ride to Cuba!

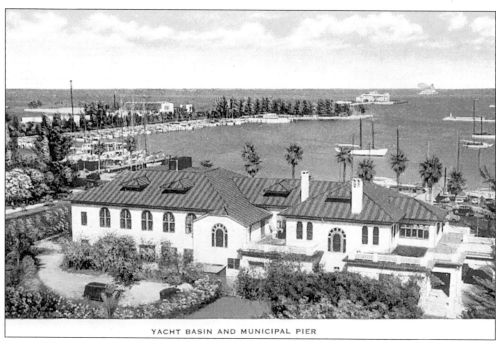

YACHT BASIN AND MUNICIPAL PIER

Major regattas were held by the St. Petersburg Yacht Club, playhouse of the rich and famous, constructed in 1916 and expanded in 1922.

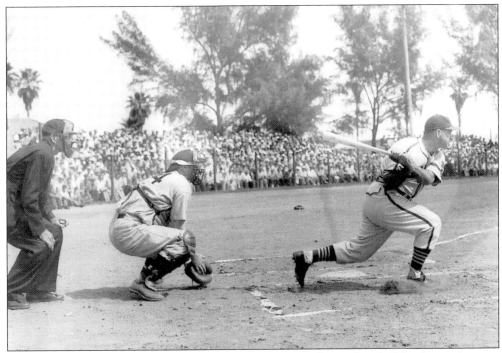

Since spring training came to St. Petersburg in 1914, major league baseball has been a big part of the Sunshine City's sports scene.

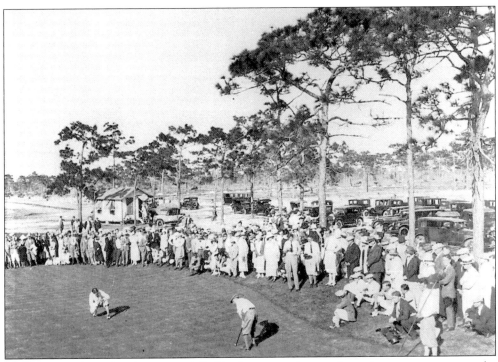

Golfing legends Walter Hagen and Bobby Jones are shown above in a tournament at the Pasadena Golf Course.

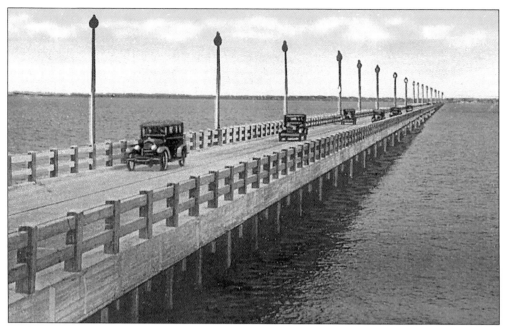

In the early days of the auto, motoring was a popular sport. Challenging roads and vehicles prone to frequent breakdowns gave it a daredevil reputation. The Gandy Bridge, shown here, connected St. Petersburg with Tampa across Tampa Bay. It was the longest automobile bridge in the world when it opened on November 20, 1924.

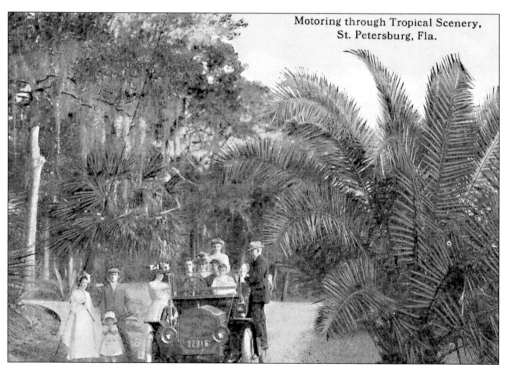

Dressed in their Sunday best, this family enjoys a ride down a sandy St. Petersburg road. The card writer describes motoring to be "the principal attraction here at the present time."

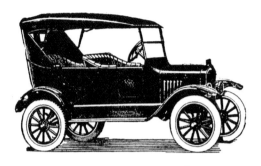 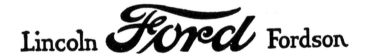
With the coming of assembly-line production during the boom era, the automobile became the transportation of the masses. By 1924, dealers such as Albright Ford were offering vehicles complete with "starter and demountable rims" for under $400!

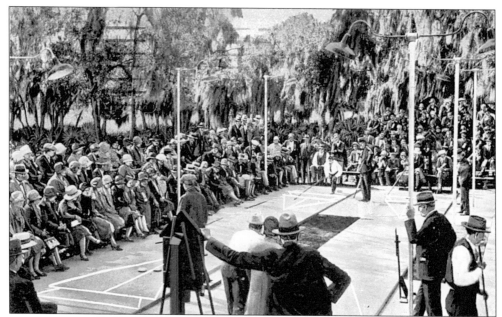

Where pro football, baseball, and basketball attract crowds in today's St. Petersburg, shuffleboard tournaments were a big draw in the early 1900s, as this 1934 scene demonstrates.

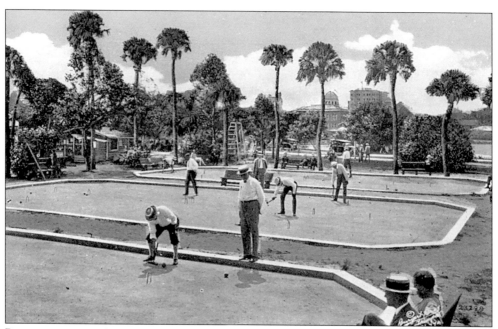

Roque, a game similar to croquet, was a favorite pastime of Sunshine City visitors.

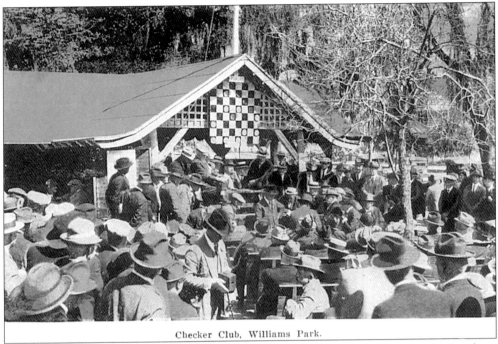

Checker Club, Williams Park.

For the more sedate and cerebral, chess and checkers were common pastimes in the Sunshine City. Williams Park is crowded here with checker players.

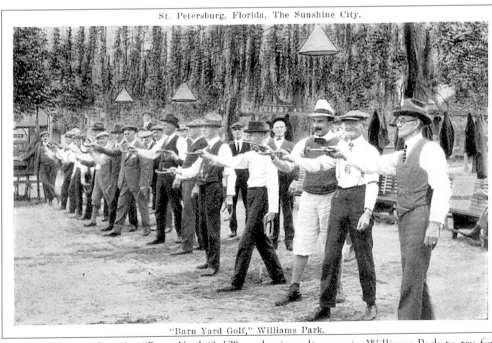

St. Petersburg, Florida, The Sunshine City.

"Barn Yard Golf," Williams Park.

A group of horseshoe (or "Barn Yard Golf") enthusiasts line up in Williams Park to try for a "ringer."

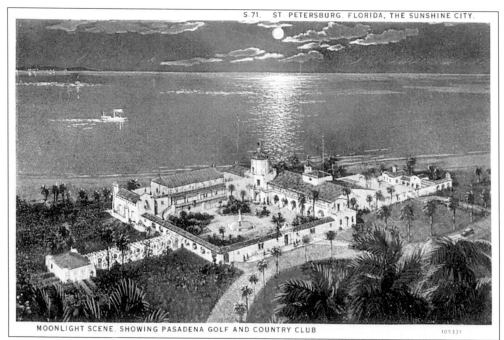

MOONLIGHT SCENE, SHOWING PASADENA GOLF AND COUNTRY CLUB.

105331

Golf reached a peak of popularity in the United States during the 1920s, and the year-round balmy climate of St. Petersburg made it an ideal place to play. The lavish Pasadena Golf and Country Club on the bay was part of Handsome Jack Taylor's Pasadena-on-the-Gulf subdivision. The complex still exists today.

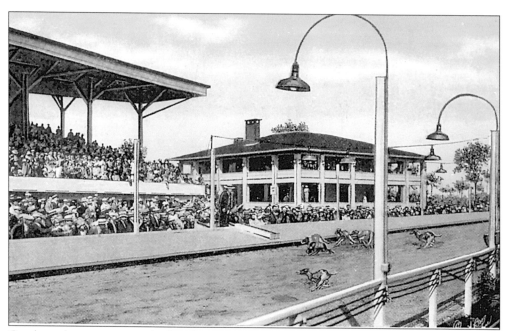

Greyhound racing came to the Sunshine City with the organization of the St. Petersburg Kennel Club in 1924. The sport took off during the 1920s, offering excitement and legalized betting. Derby Lane, shown here, was the world's oldest greyhound track.

Seven

RESIDENCES

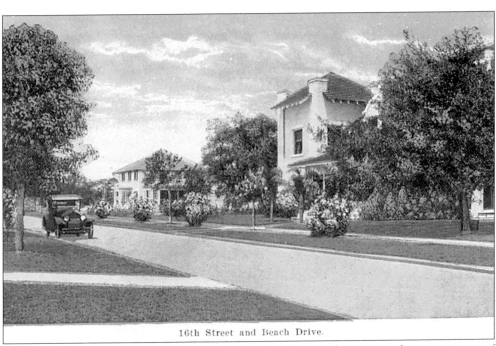

16th Street and Beach Drive.

Early St. Petersburg was known for beautiful residential areas, featuring a pleasant mixture of distinctive home styles clothed in tropical verdure. The homes were well built by prominent developers and many still exist in the city's beautifully preserved neighborhoods. Real estate agents were active in St. Petersburg during the boom era, selling visitors on becoming residents. Fortunes were made (and many later lost) in the booming real estate arena.

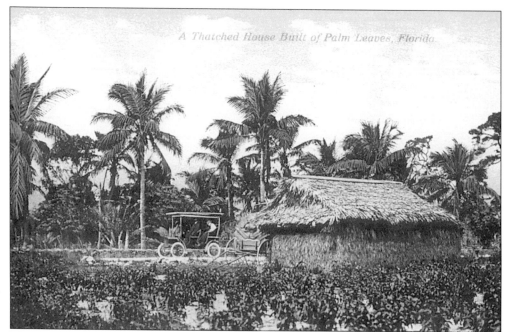

The earliest Florida homes were simple shanties constructed of natural materials, such as thatched palm leaves. Homes of this type, often "fishing shanties," were quickly displaced during St. Petersburg's construction boom.

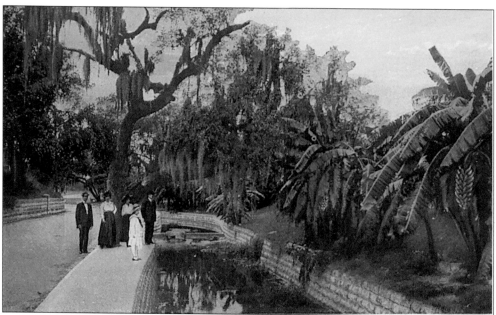

Roser Park was the brainchild of developer C.M. Roser, who began with the intention of developing a few lots along Brooker's Creek. The idea grew and the result was the picturesque Roser Park neighborhood, a community of distinctive homes designed around the natural contours of the landscape. Roser had been an owner of the Newton Biscuit Co. and developed the Fig Newton.

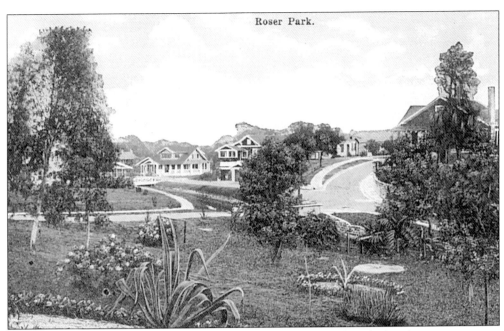

Roser Park.

Roser took full advantage of the ravines and hills in the area and worked with nature to create a most attractive community setting.

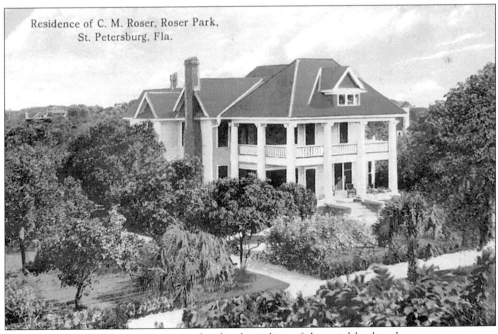

Residence of C. M. Roser, Roser Park, St. Petersburg, Fla.

Developer Roser built his mansion to be the showplace of the neighborhood.

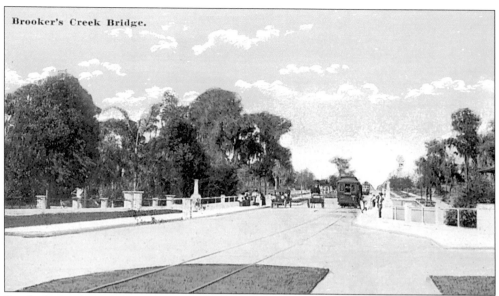

Brooker's Creek Bridge spanned the Roser Park development, providing easy access to the neighborhood by foot, auto, or streetcar.

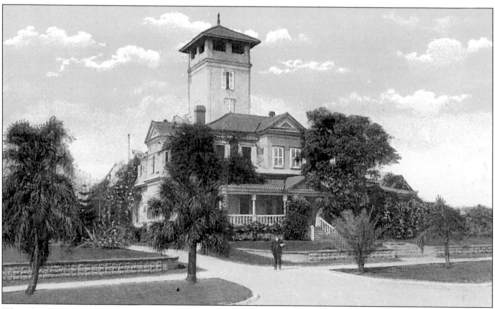

This distinctive mansion at Second Avenue South and Fourth Street was the residence of Edwin H. Tomlinson, a wealthy St. Petersburg philanthropist. Tomlinson built the tower adjacent to his home in 1900 for the use of his friend Guglielmo Marconi, the inventor of the telegraph, in conducting wireless experiments. However, Marconi never made it to Florida, and the tower was heavily damaged by lightning in 1901. Congressman Joseph Sibley of Pennsylvania purchased the house in 1905.

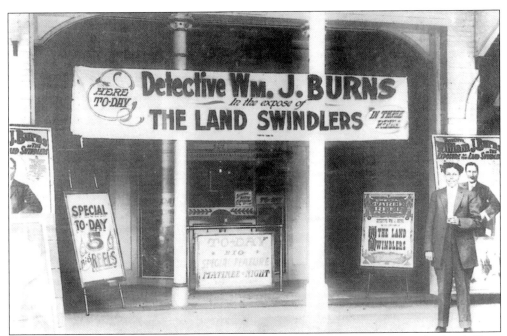

The relentless real estate speculation of the boom era brought the opportunity for fraud. Here, the Royal Palm Theater presents the three-reel feature expose film *The Land Swindlers*. Theater owner Bill Carpenter, "The Alligator Man," is standing at right.

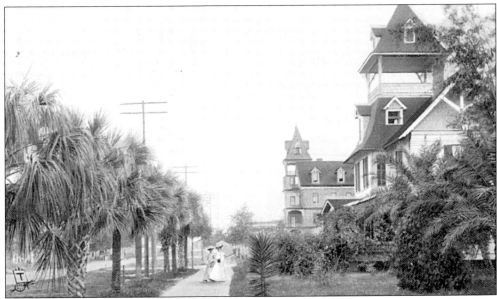

The Old Northeast Neighborhood, featured over the next several pages, is a National Historic Landmark extending from Tampa Bay west to Fourth Street North, and from Fifth to Twenty-third Avenue North. The area encompasses 160 blocks and contains over 3,500 restored homes and structures. The earliest homes in the area were large wooden structures, often with Victorian cupolas, as shown in this 1909 view looking down Second Street. Most homes of this style are now gone.

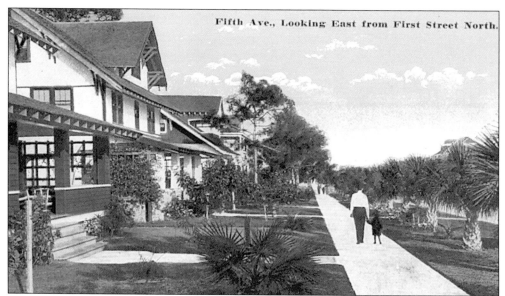

Homes in the Old Northeast Neighborhood today represent an eclectic mixture of styles that were constructed in the boom period by prominent St. Petersburg developers such as J.C. Hamlett and C. Perry Snell of Snell Arcade fame.

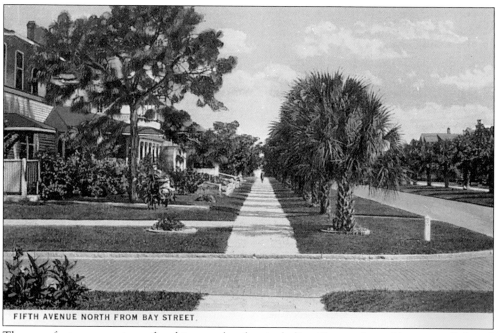

The area features a variety of architectural styles, including Queen Anne Victorian, Colonial Revival, Mediterranean Revival, Craftsman (bought from Sears catalogs), and Prairie.

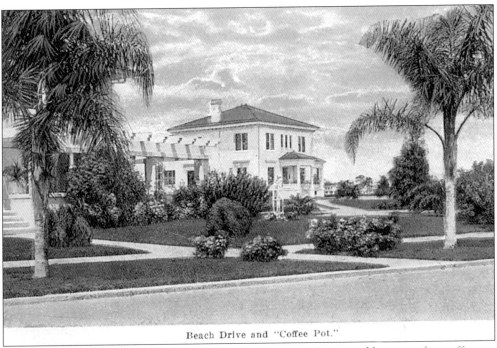

Beach Drive and "Coffee Pot."

Grand mansions and spacious villas faced Coffee Pot Bayou (so named because of its coffee-pot shape when viewed from above).

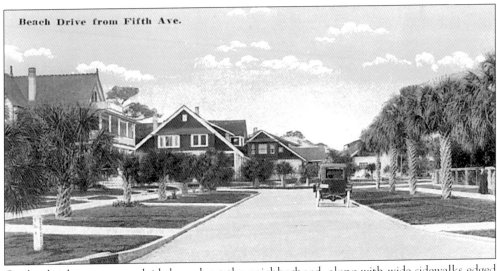

Beach Drive from Fifth Ave.

Quality-brick streets were laid throughout the neighborhood, along with wide sidewalks edged with plenty of greenery. This view was taken at Fifth Avenue North and Beach Drive.

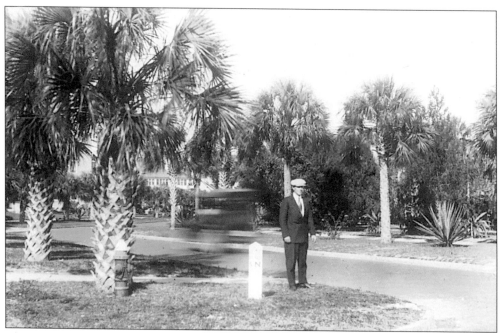

This photo of "Dan at foot of Fifth Avenue North and Beach Drive, Winter 1920–1921" shows the park-like tropical setting of the area.

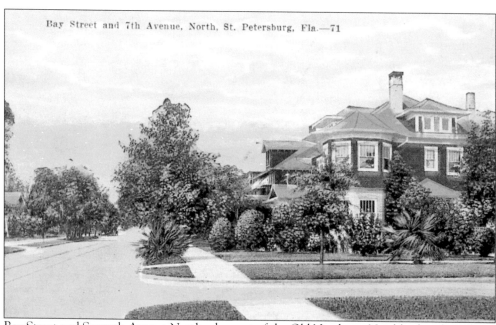

Bay Street and Seventh Avenue North, also part of the Old Northeast Neighborhood, are lined with the individually designed handcrafted homes typical of the area.

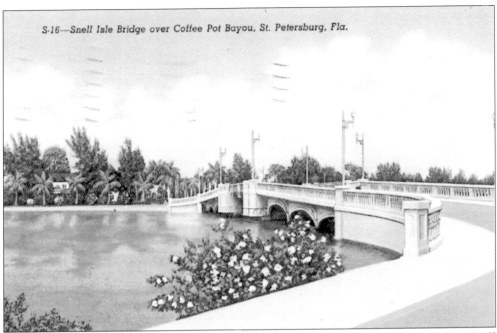

This masonry bridge, built in 1936, crossed Coffee Pot Bayou to the exclusive Snell Isle development.

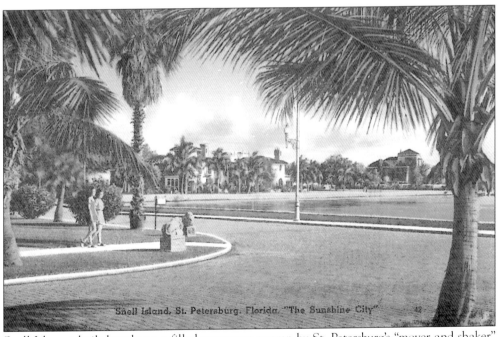

Snell Isle was built largely on a filled mangrove swamp by St. Petersburg's "mover and shaker" developer Perry Snell. It was widely considered to be Snell's "crown jewel" development, and he lined the handsome brick streets with Mediterranean Revival–style mansions of stucco and red tiled roofs.

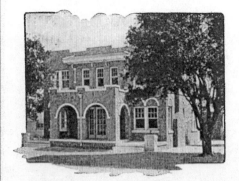

A distinctive Florida atmosphere pervades this Schooley-Murphy home at Pasadena.

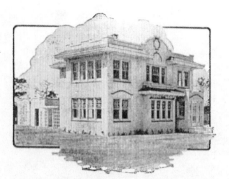

A Schooley-Murphy hollow tile stucco two-tone Spanish type Euclid Place home.

Builders of Fine Homes

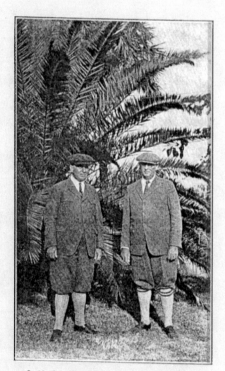

S. V. Schooley, left; P. M. Murphy, right.

The Schooley-Murphy homes in Pasadena, Euclid Place and North Shore have gained for St. Petersburg an enviable reputation as a city of beautiful homes.

Within the past two years we have built and sold over 200 residences valued at more than three million dollars.

Schooley-Murphy homes are distinctive in design, elegant in appearance and built to endure.

Schooley-Murphy Company

Builders of Fine Homes

St. Petersburg, Florida

St. Petersburg was fortunate to have attracted a number of fine developers who left a legacy of beautiful, quality-built homes in attractive settings. This ad promoted the Schooley-Murphy Company that built homes in Pasadena, Euclid Place, and the North Shore, which are still premier St. Petersburg addresses.

Lumber Headquarters for St. Petersburg

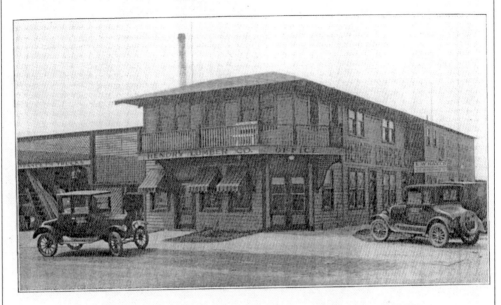

Our yards are full of the best grade of every kind of lumber, sills, flooring, lath, sash, doors, window frames, moulding and the finest pieces for interior finish; in fact, any kind of wood you want.

—almost every piece of material necessary, from the foundation to the roof, to build a good house can be found in our yards.

When it comes to painting "Red Spot" will answer all your requirements. This paint is particularly adapted to Florida's climate.

And for the roof. "Hendry's No-Curl Shingles" or "Leaktite Roll Roofing," both private brands, are made especially for Florida homes.

Individual home builders and contractors alike can save, and are saving, time, money and worry by coming direct to "Lumber Headquarters" for their building materials.

Our fleet of trucks and large corps of trained workmen are here to serve you.

The Hendry Lumber Company

W. A. HENDRY, Manager

Phone 7795

Fourteenth Street and Second Avenue North   St. Petersburg, Florida

Many businesses sprang up during the boom era to service the housing industry. This 1926 ad for the Hendry Lumber Company offered "the best grade of every kind of lumber, sills, flooring, lath, sash, doors, window frames, molding, and the finest pieces for interior finish."

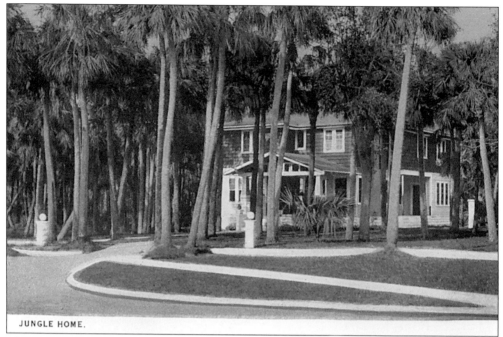

JUNGLE HOME.

The Davista (later Pasadena) and Jungle developments were started by H. Walter Fuller with his son Walter P. Fuller in the early to mid-1910s. Carved from a literal jungle on the eastern shores of Boca Ciega Bay, the developments featured large, mansion-size homes in a planned community setting.

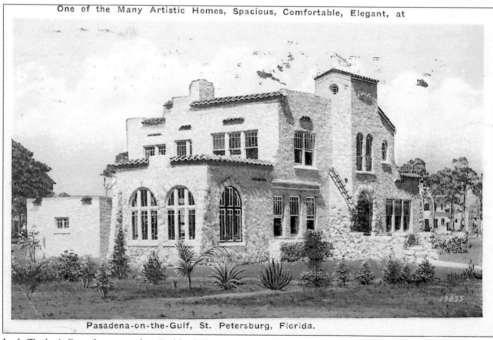

One of the Many Artistic Homes, Spacious, Comfortable, Elegant, at

Pasadena-on-the-Gulf, St. Petersburg, Florida.

Jack Taylor's Pasadena-on-the-Gulf subdivision complemented his lavish Rolyat Hotel, featuring showcase homes of the highest quality materials and workmanship.

Eight

THE BEACH

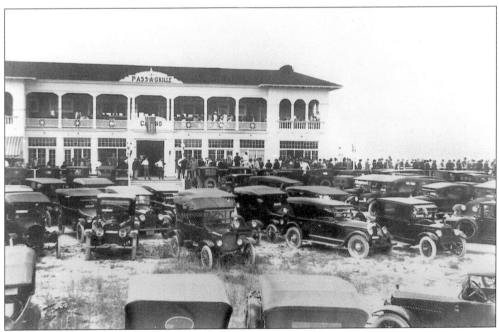

Surprisingly, the Gulf beaches were largely undeveloped in the early resort era; vacationers preferred the security and easy access of the bay front and gardens. In the St. Petersburg beach areas, a few casinos (dancing and bathing pavilions) were the earliest developments, along with the showplace Don CeSar Hotel. Motels of the "mom and pop" variety followed in the 1930s and 1940s. The extensive beach development that we know today did not actually occur until the 1950s, but early tourists did enjoy visiting the beach, originally by ferry and then by motorcar after the bridge was built. The Pass-a-Grille Casino, shown here in an early view, later became the Pass-a-Grille Beach Hotel.

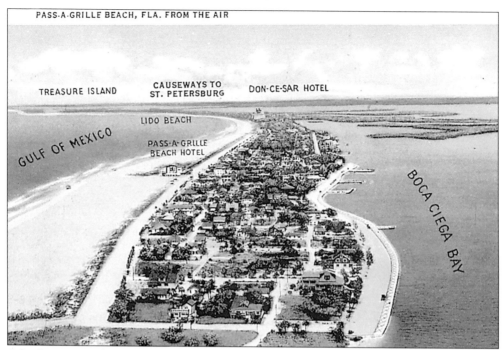

PASS-A-GRILLE BEACH, FLA. FROM THE AIR

TREASURE ISLAND   CAUSEWAYS TO ST. PETERSBURG   DON-CE-SAR HOTEL

LIDO BEACH

GULF OF MEXICO

PASS-A-GRILLE BEACH HOTEL

BOCA CIEGA BAY

A bird's-eye view shows Pass-a-Grille from the southern tip of the island.

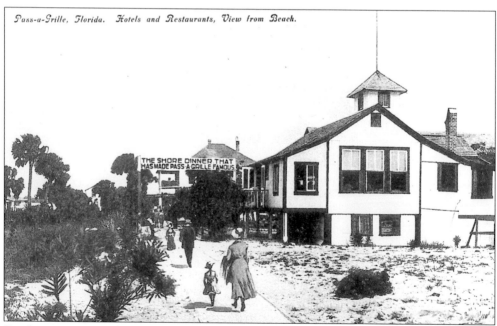

Pass-a-Grille, Florida. Hotels and Restaurants, View from Beach.

THE SHORE DINNER THAT HAS MADE PASS-A-GRILLE FAMOUS.

Beach restaurants took advantage of the plentiful fish population in the Gulf, making seafood dinners a prime attraction.

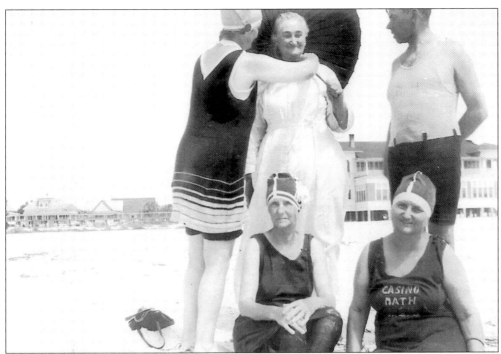

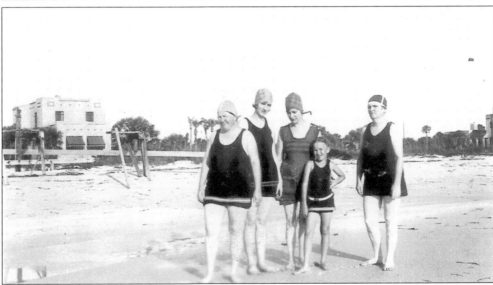

In the above images, "bathing beauties" check out the beach at Pass-a-Grille.

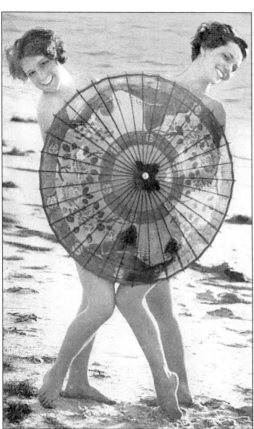

Photos like this one, considered risque for the time, helped publicize the beach as a place for fun and relaxation.

These children appear to be having a grand time in the sand.

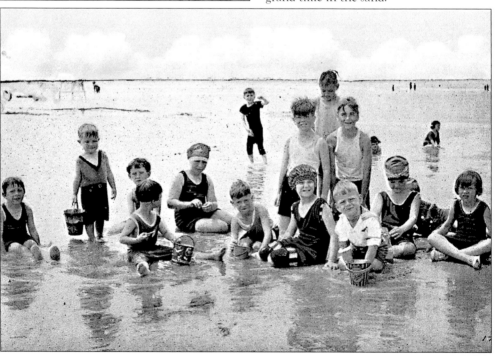

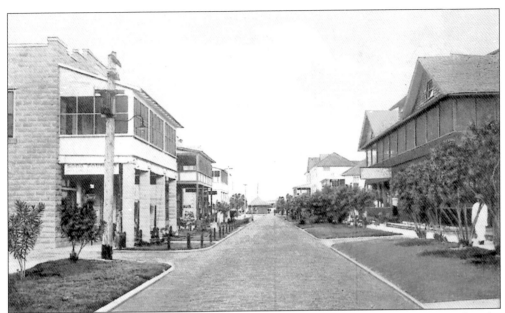

The earliest developed beach community in the St. Petersburg area was Pass-a-Grille. Before the bridge to the mainland was built in 1919, the only access to the town was by ferry. The message on this card reads "Pass-a-Grille is on an island. You go on car to Gulf Port and across the bay in a boat." Pass-a-Grille, on the southern tip of the beach strip, has been largely preserved in its original state. Note the brick streets.

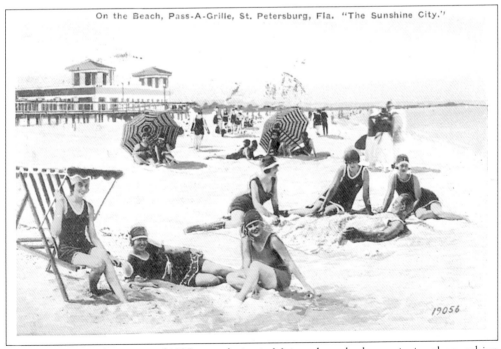

This card, sent in the winter of 1925 to a relative in Maine, shows bathers enjoying the sunshine at Pass-a-Grille. The postcard was an invaluable form of publicity that helped keep Sunshine City tourism booming.

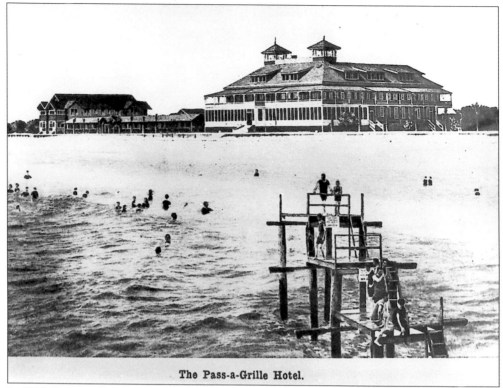

The Pass-a-Grille Hotel.

In 1913, St. Petersburg developer H. Walter Fuller purchased the elegant La Plaza Hotel, turning it into the expensive and "luxurious" Pass-a-Grille. The hotel burned in 1922. To the left is the Butler House, at one time considered the finest on the beaches.

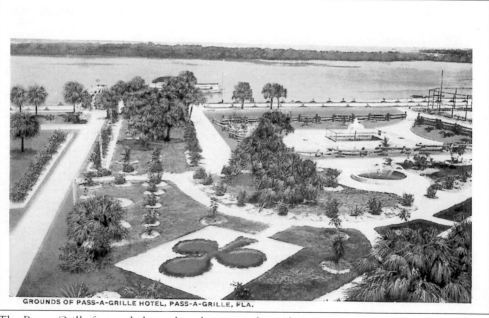

GROUNDS OF PASS-A-GRILLE HOTEL, PASS-A-GRILLE, FLA.

The Pass-a-Grille featured planned gardens on its bay side.

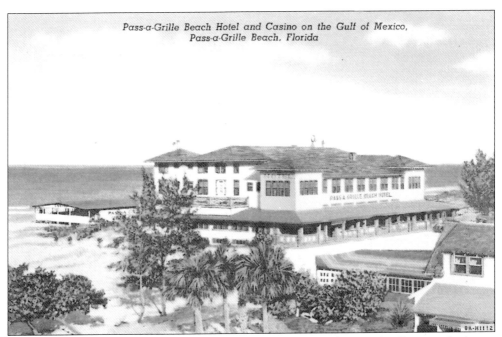

Pass-a-Grille Beach Hotel and Casino on the Gulf of Mexico,
Pass-a-Grille Beach, Florida

The Pass-a-Grille Hotel name, with "Beach" added, was passed on to the Casino, which was renovated to become the Pass-a-Grille Beach Hotel and Casino in the early 1920s. The hotel served guests for several decades until it succumbed to fire in 1967.

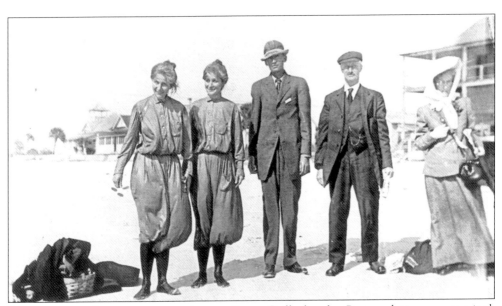

Victorian picnickers enjoy an outing on Pass-a-Grille beach. Coat and tie were required, of course.

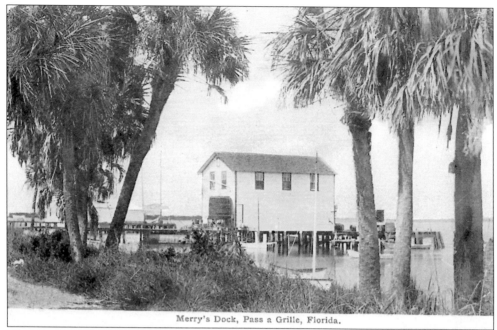

Merry's Dock, Pass a Grille, Florida.

This structure, built in 1902 by Joseph E. Merry on the dock at Eighth and Pass-a-Grille Way, housed the first store on the Gulf beaches.

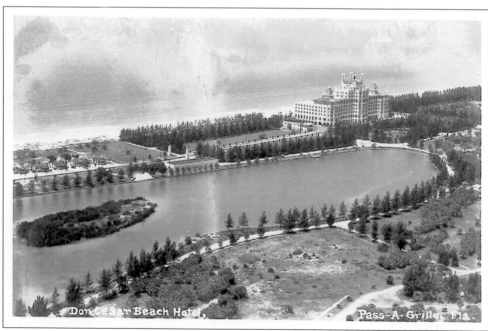

Don CeSar Beach Hotel, Pass-A-Grille, Fla.

The showplace of the beach during the boom era was the grand Don CeSar, which appears almost isolated in this 1920s photo.

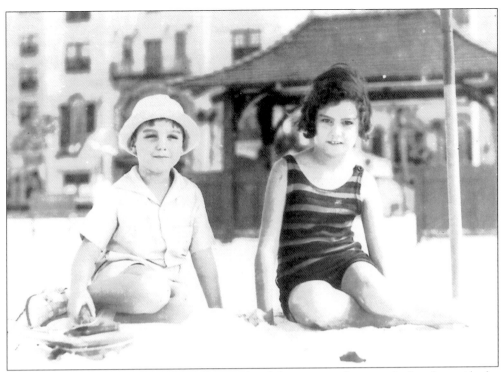

Robert E. Lee IV, the grandson of the famous Confederate general, enjoys the beach outside the Don CeSar with his sister Mary Walker Lee.

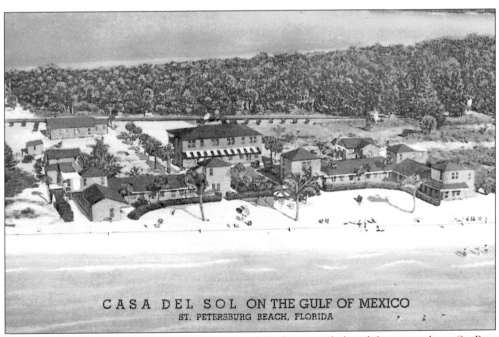

CASA DEL SOL ON THE GULF OF MEXICO
ST. PETERSBURG BEACH, FLORIDA

The Casa del Sol (Castle in the Sun) was one of the larger early beachfront motels on St. Pete Beach. Its low rambling style was common while beachfront property was cheap.

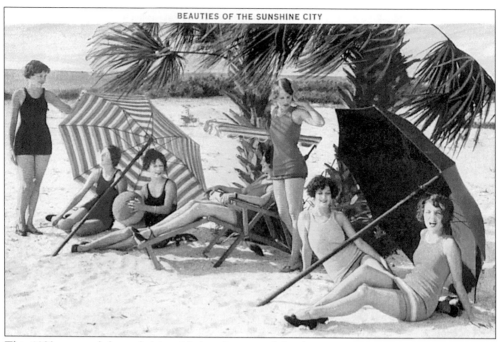

This 1933 postcard shows fashionable beach attire of the day.

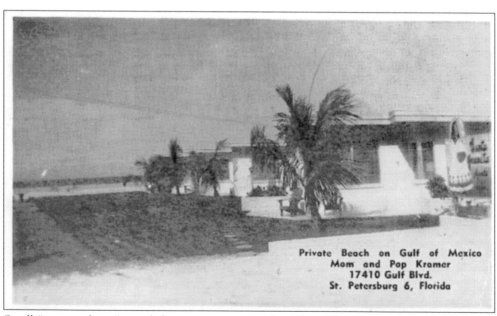

Private Beach on Gulf of Mexico
Mom and Pop Kramer
17410 Gulf Blvd.
St. Petersburg 6, Florida

Small "mom and pop" motels began to appear in the 1930s. This one on St. Pete Beach was operated by "Mom and Pop Kramer."

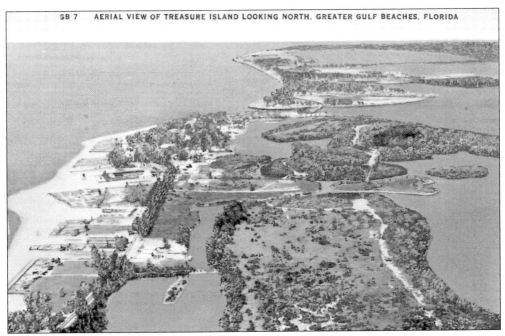

Treasure Island was still largely undeveloped as late as the 1940s.

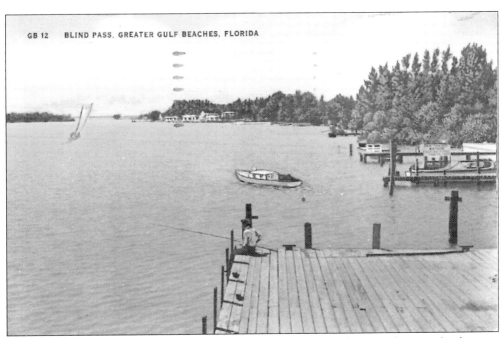

BLIND PASS, GREATER GULF BEACHES, FLORIDA

Blind Pass appears tranquil and sparsely populated here. The Blind Pass Bridge is in the distance at upper left.

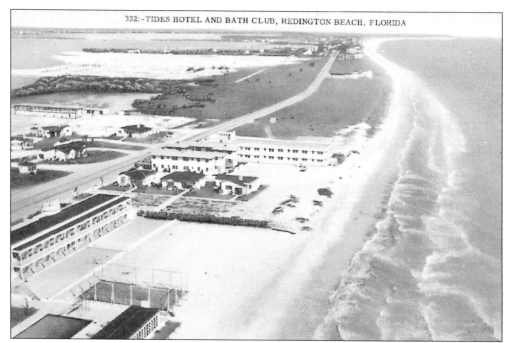

The Tides Hotel at Redington Beach opened in 1939 as the largest resort on the upper beaches. A sign of the end of the Depression era, it was the first major hotel project in southern Pinellas County since the mid-1920s. The hotel continued operation until the late 1990s, when it was replaced by the luxury Tides Condominiums.

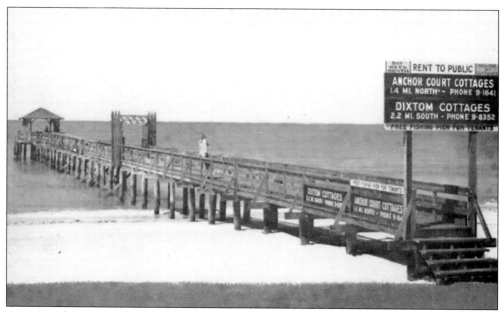

Accommodations at the beach were mainly cottages and small motels. Two cottage sites are advertised above, at the Indian Rocks Pier, along with the enticement "free fishing pier for tenants."